The Indispensability of Mathematics

The Indispensability of Mathematics

MARK COLYVAN

OXFORD

UNIVERSITY PRESS

2001

OXFORD
UNIVERSITY PRESS

Oxford   New York

Athens   Auckland   Bangkok   Bogotá   Buenos Aires   Calcutta
Cape Town   Chennai   Dar es Salaam   Delhi   Florence   Hong Kong   Istanbul
Karachi   Kuala Lumpur   Madrid   Melbourne   Mexico City   Mumbai   Nairobi
Paris   São Paulo   Shanghai   Singapore   Taipei   Tokyo   Toronto   Warsaw

and associated companies in
Berlin   Ibadan

Published by Oxford University Press, Inc.
198 Madison Avenue, New York, New York 10016

Oxford is a registered trademark of Oxford University Press

Library of Congress Cataloging-in-Publication Data
Colyvan, Mark.
The indispensability of mathematics / Mark Colyvan.
p. cm.
Includes bibliographical references and index.
ISBN 0-19-513754-X
1. Mathematics—Philosophy.   I. Title.
QA8.4 .C65 2000
510—dc21   00-037346

1 3 5 7 9 8 6 4 2

Printed in the United States of America
on acid-free paper

Acknowledgments

I'd like to thank Jody Azzouni, Alan Baker, Paul Benacerraf, John Bigelow, Brian Birchall, James Chase, Colin Cheyne, Stephen Ferguson, Hartry Field, Peter Forrest, Jay Garfield, Philip Gerrans, Ian Gold, Geoffrey Hellman, Frank Jackson, Drew Khlentzos, Keith Lehrer, Bernard Linsky, Penelope Maddy, Peter Menzies, Bob Meyer, Alan Musgrave, Daniel Nolan, Alex Oliver, Graham Oppy, Philip Pettit, Michael Potter, W. V. Quine, Helen Regan, Mike Resnik, Peter Roeper, Gideon Rosen, David Ryan, Jack Smart, and Ed Zalta. All of these people have made significant intellectual contributions to this work.

This book draws upon material which has been published elsewhere, so I'd like to thank the relevant publishers for their permission to use that material again here. The copyright for previously published material remains with the relevant journals. Much of chapter 3 comes from "Can the Eleatic Principle be Justified?" (Colyvan (1998c)) in *The Canadian Journal of Philosophy*. Much of chapter 4 (and some of chapter 1) comes from "Confirmation Theory and Indispensability" (Colyvan (1999c)) in *Philosophical Studies*. Chapter 5 draws heavily on "In Defence of Indispensability" (Colyvan (1998a)) in *Philosophia Mathematica* and also on my review of Penelope Maddy's *Naturalism in Mathematics* (Colyvan (1999a)) in *Mind*. Chapter 6 draws upon "Contrastive Empiricism and Indispensability" (Colyvan (1999b)) in *Erkenntnis* and "Conceptual Contingency and Abstract Existence" (Colyvan (2000)) in *The Philosophical Quarterly*. Chapter 7 draws on "Is Platonism a Bad Bet?" (Colyvan (1998b)) in *The Australasian Journal of Philosophy*.

Hobart, Tasmania   M. C.
October 2000

Contents

The Indispensability of Mathematics

1

Mathematics and Its Applications

For some time now ontological debates in the philosophy of mathematics have been dominated by three arguments. The first of these is the Benacerraf indeterminacy objection to the natural numbers being identified with sets.[1] The second argument, also due to Benacerraf, is the well-known epistemological problem for Platonism. That is, if mathematical objects such as functions, numbers, and sets have mind-independent, though admittedly abstract, existence, how is it that we have knowledge of them (Benacerraf (1973))? (This is often referred to as *the problem of naturalising mathematical epistemology*.) The third argument is the Quinean argument that mathematical entities are indispensable to our best physical theories and therefore share the ontological status of scientific entities. The first two of these arguments are taken to raise problems for the position called Platonism or mathematical realism, while the third is usually taken to be an argument *for* Platonism; perhaps, as Hartry Field suggests, "the only non-question-begging" argument for Platonism (Field, 1980, p. 4).

Although I will return to the two Benacerraf problems in the final chapter, for the most part I'll be concerned with the indispensability argument. In particular, I will be defending this argument against some of its recent critics. Before discussing the indispensability argument in more detail, though, some preliminaries are in order. Since the argument is supposed to have serious implications for the debate about realism and anti-realism

---

[1] For example, should we identify the natural number three with von Neumann's $\{\emptyset, \{\emptyset\}, \{\emptyset, \{\emptyset\}\}\}$ or with Zermelo's $\{\{\{\emptyset\}\}\}$? See Benacerraf (1965) for further details.

in mathematics, I need to say a little about what I take realism and anti-realism to be, and also what I take this debate to be about in the case of mathematics.

1.1 Realism and Anti-realism in Mathematics

There are many different ways to characterise realism and anti-realism in mathematics. Perhaps the most common way is as a thesis about the existence or non-existence of mathematical entities. Thus, according to this conception of realism, mathematical entities such as functions, numbers, and sets have mind- and language-independent existence or, as it is also commonly expressed, we *discover* rather than invent mathematical theories (which are taken to be a body of facts about the relevant mathematical objects). This is usually called *metaphysical realism*. Anti-realism, then, is the position that mathematical entities do not enjoy mind-independent existence or, alternatively, we *invent* rather than discover mathematical theories. According to this characterisation, a realist believes that Fermat's Last Theorem[2] was true before Wiles's proof and, indeed, even before Fermat first thought of his now famous theorem. This is because, according to the realist, the integers exist independently of our knowledge of them and Fermat's theorem is a fact about them.

Another common characterisation of realism is via truth. For instance Michael Dummett says that realism is "the belief that statements of the disputed class possess an objective truth-value, independently of our means of knowing it: they are true or false in virtue of a reality existing independently of us" (Dummett, 1978a, p. 146).[3] This is usually called *semantic realism*. Hilary Putnam, another who prefers this way of characterising realism, points out that, according to this view, it is possible to be a mathematical realist without being committed to mathematical objects—realism is about objectivity, not objects (Putnam, 1979a, pp. 69–70). For example, suppose mathematical discourse is reinterpreted so that it does not refer to mathematical objects and this reinterpreted discourse is true or false

---

[2] This theorem states that there are only trivial integer solutions of the equation $x^n + y^n = z^n$ when $n > 2$. It is called "Fermat's Last Theorem" because Fermat noted in the margin of a book that he had a proof of this but that the margin was too small to contain it. Fermat never produced a proof and, what is more, it seems exceptionally unlikely that he had a proof, given the difficulty of the proof first produced by Andrew Wiles in 1993. See Singh (1997) for further details.

[3] Others, such as Geoffrey Sayre-McCord (1988), also require that some of the statements in the disputed class be true, for otherwise fictionalists turn out to be realists.

independently of our knowledge of it. Such a position satisfies Dummett's characterisation of realism, and yet there are no entities peculiar to mathematics. Indeed, Putnam's own modal-structuralist account of mathematics is a nice example of a realist view of mathematics that has no mathematical objects.[4]

Putnam's claim that it is the objectivity of mathematics that is really the issue is surely correct for a great many contexts, but not when one is doing metaphysics! Certainly one reason many philosophers and mathematicians find the view that mathematical objects exist appealing is that it does provide mathematics with the desired objectivity. For instance, as Penelope Maddy points out (1996b, pp. 68–69), Kurt Gödel was drawn to mathematical realism for this very reason: Platonism purported to provide the independent questions of mathematics with objective answers.[5] If this were all there was at issue, then Putnam's account of realism would suffice, but objectivity is not the *only* issue. The important question in the ontology of mathematics is: Do mathematical objects exist? I take this question to be interesting and worth pursuing. The Dummett/Putnam characterisation of realism and anti-realism, however, does not address this question.[6]

Since, in this work, my interests are metaphysical, I will be concerned with metaphysical realism, not semantic realism. I will, however, speak only of *realism*, by which I will mean *metaphysical* realism. I should stress that I am *not* presupposing that metaphysical realism is the correct account of realism—my use of "realism" to mean "metaphysical realism" is merely terminological.[7]

While on matters terminological, I should also point out that, in keeping with most of the modern literature in the area, I will use the terms 'mathematical realism' and 'Platonism' interchangeably. So I take Platonism to be the view that mathematical objects exist and, what is more, that their existence is not mind or language dependent. I also take it that according to Platonism, mathematical statements are true or false in virtue of the properties of these mathematical objects. I do not mean to imply anything more than this. I do not, for instance, intend Platonism to imply

---

[4] On this view, mathematical claims are reinterpreted as modal claims. For instance, the claim that numbers exist becomes the claim that ω-sequences are (mathematically) possible. See Putnam (1967) for further details.

[5] Indeed, Maddy too has much sympathy with this style of motivation.

[6] This is not to say, however, that the Dummett/Putnam account is without merit. You might be inclined to think that what is important in realism *is* captured by Dummett's characterisation, but that questions concerning ontology are somewhat independent of issues of realism.

[7] The issue of explicating the best or correct account of realism is far too large to do justice to here. See Wright (1992) for an interesting discussion of this topic.

that mathematical objects are causally inert, that they are not located in space-time, or that they exist necessarily. Although such views are *typically* endorsed by Platonists, such endorsement is by no means universal. For example, Penelope Maddy (1990a) and John Bigelow (1988) have both put forward accounts of mathematics, which they describe as Platonist accounts, in which mathematical objects are located in space-time and are part of the causal nexus. Others propose accounts where mathematical objects exist contingently.[8] These accounts all postulate mathematical objects and, from an ontological point of view, this is what matters. I will thus use the term 'Platonism' to include them all.

Given this characterisation of mathematical realism or Platonism, we can reasonably ask about anti-realist accounts of mathematics. Clearly any account that denies that mathematical objects exist is anti-realist. I shall call such anti-realist positions *nominalist*. There is also a second anti-realist position. According to this view, mathematical objects exist but they are mind- or language-dependent. I agree with Hartry Field (1989, pp. 1–2) that this last position is of little interest. The important question is whether mind- and language-independent mathematical objects exist or not. Having noted this second position, I will now largely ignore it. I will thus speak of Platonism and nominalism as the two viable positions.[9]

There are various Platonist and nominalist strategies in the philosophy of mathematics, some of which we will meet later in the book. Each of these has its own particular strengths and weaknesses. As I've already mentioned, Platonist accounts of mathematics generally have the problems of providing an adequate epistemology for mathematics and of explaining the apparent indeterminacy of number terms. On the other hand, nominalist accounts generally have trouble providing an adequate treatment of the wide and varied applications of mathematics in the empirical sciences. There is also the challenge for nominalism to provide a uniform semantics for mathematics and other discourse (Benacerraf (1973)).[10] It might be useful at this stage to outline a few of the different strategies encountered in the literature.

An important nominalist response to these arguments is fictionalism. A fictionalist about mathematics believes that mathematical statements are,

---

[8] As we shall see, I endorse such a view.

[9] If you wish, you can consider my sense of nominalism here to include the second anti-realist position by thinking of nominalism as the view that no mind-independent mathematical objects exist.

[10] Although this last challenge receives less attention than the other three arguments, I don't think that this lack of attention signifies that this challenge is of less importance. A believable nominalist account must provide an account of the semantics of mathematical discourse that is not ad hoc.

by and large, false. According to the fictionalist, mathematical statements are "true in the story of mathematics" but this does not amount to truth simpliciter. Fictionalists take their lead from some standard semantics for literary fiction. On many accounts of literary fiction "Sherlock Holmes is a detective" is false (because there is no such person as Sherlock Holmes), but it is "true in the stories of Conan Doyle." The mathematical fiction-alist takes sentences such as "seven is prime" to be false (because there is no such entity as seven) but "true in the story of mathematics." The fic-tionalist thus provides a distinctive response to the challenge of providing a uniform semantics—all the usually accepted statements of mathematics are false.[11] The problem of explaining the applicability of mathematics is more involved, and I will leave a discussion of this to chapter 4, where I consider in more detail one particular version of fictionalism due to Hartry Field.

In recent times many Platonist strategies have responded to the episte-mological challenge by placing mathematical objects firmly in the physical realm. Thus Penelope Maddy in *Realism in Mathematics* (1990a) argued that we can see sets. When we see six eggs in a carton we are seeing *the set* of six eggs. This account provides mathematics with an epistemology consistent with other areas of knowledge by giving up one of the core doc-trines of traditional Platonism—that mathematical entities are abstract. In response to the apparent indeterminacy of the reduction of numbers to sets, one popular Platonist strategy is to identify a given natural number with a certain position in *any* ω-sequence. Thus, it doesn't matter that three can be represented as $\{\{\{\emptyset\}\}\}$ in Zermelo's ω-sequence and $\{\emptyset, \{\emptyset\}, \{\emptyset, \{\emptyset\}\}\}$ in von Neumann's ω-sequence. What is important according to this account is that the structural properties are identical. This view is usually called *structuralism* since it is the structures that are important, not the items that constitute the structures.[12]

These are not meant to be anything more than cursory sketches of some of the available positions. Some of these positions will arise again later, but for now I will be content with these sketches and move on to discuss in-dispensability arguments and how these arguments are supposed to deliver mathematical realism.

---

[11] This is not quite right. Since fictionalists take the domain of quantification to be empty, they claim that all existentially quantified statements (and statements about what are apparently denoting terms) are false, but that all universally quantified sentences are true. So, for example, "there is an even prime number" is taken to be false while "every number has a successor" is taken to be true.

[12] See, for example, Resnik (1981; 1982; 1997), Hellman (1989), and Shapiro (1997).

1.2   Indispensability Arguments

1.2.1   Introducing Indispensability Arguments

One of the most intriguing features of mathematics is its applicability to empirical science. Every branch of science draws upon large and often diverse portions of mathematics, from the use of Lie groups in quantum mechanics to the use of differential geometry in cosmology. It's not only the physical sciences that avail themselves of the services of mathematics either. Biology, for instance, makes extensive use of difference equations and statistics. The role mathematics plays in these theories is also varied. Not only does mathematics help with empirical predictions, it allows elegant and economical statement of many theories. Indeed, so important is the language of mathematics that it is hard to imagine how some theories could even be stated without it. Furthermore, looking at the world through mathematical eyes has, on more than one occasion, facilitated enormous breakthroughs in science.[13]

That mathematics should be so suited to such a great range of tasks is in itself quite remarkable. The mathematical physicist Eugene Wigner, in a rather famous article on the applications of mathematics (1960), calls this the "unreasonable effectiveness of mathematics" and speaks almost mystically of this as a "miracle." I'll have very little to say about *why* mathematics is so remarkably useful in such a huge variety of applications. This is not because such questions are uninteresting or that they are easily answered. On the contrary, I believe that explaining the applicability of mathematics is one of the most perplexing issues in the philosophy of mathematics—it's just that a discussion of this issue would take us too far from the task at hand and, what is more, such a discussion would have little bearing on this task.[14] Instead, I take as a starting point the simple, undeniable fact that mathematics *has* such applications. In this work I'm concerned largely with indispensability arguments, and these arguments purport to yield conclusions about ontology based on this simple, undeniable fact.

An indispensability argument, as Hartry Field points out, "is an argument that we should believe a certain claim ... because doing so is indispensable for certain purposes (which the argument then details)" (Field, 1989, p. 14). Clearly the strength of the argument depends crucially on what the as-yet unspecified purpose is. For instance, few would find the

---

[13] For example, Paul Dirac was led to the discovery of anti-matter by the equations of relativistic quantum mechanics. I'll discuss this example in more detail in section 4.4.2.

[14] See Wigner (1960) and Steiner (1989; 1995; 1998) for further discussion on the applicability of mathematics.

following argument persuasive: We should believe that whites are morally superior to blacks because doing so is indispensable for the purpose of justifying black slavery. Similarly, few would be convinced by the argument that we ought to believe that God exists because to do so is indispensable to the purpose of enjoying a healthy religious life. The "certain purposes" of which Field speaks must be chosen very carefully. Although the two arguments just mentioned count as indispensability arguments, they are implausible because "enjoying a healthy religious life" and "justifying black slavery" are *not* the right sort of purposes to ensure the cogency of the respective arguments. This raises the very interesting question: Which purposes *are* the right sort for cogent arguments?

I know of no easy answer to this question, but fortunately an answer is not required for a defence of the class of indispensability arguments with which I am concerned. I will restrict my attention largely to arguments that address indispensability to *our best scientific theories*. I will argue that this *is* the right sort of purpose for cogent indispensability arguments. I will also be concerned primarily with indispensability arguments in which the "certain claim" of which Field speaks is an existence claim. We may thus take a scientific indispensability argument to rest upon the following major premise:

Argument 1 (Scientific Indispensability Argument) *If apparent reference to some entity (or class of entities) ξ is indispensable to our best scientific theories, then we ought to believe in the existence of ξ.*

In this formulation, the purpose, if you like, is that of doing science. This is a rather ill-defined purpose, and I deliberately leave it ill defined for the moment. But to give an example of one particularly important scientific indispensability argument, with a well-defined purpose, consider the argument that takes providing explanations of empirical facts as its purpose. I'll call such an argument an *explanatory* indispensability argument.

Although indispensability arguments are typically associated with realism about mathematical objects, it's important to realise that they do have a much wider usage. What is more, this wider usage is fairly uncontroversial. To see this, we need only consider a couple of examples of explanatory indispensability arguments used for non-mathematical purposes.

Before the theory of evolution was developed, it was generally considered that the best explanation for many empirical facts about the various life forms on this planet was that these life forms were designed by God. Such an argument is a type of indispensability argument. Although it is now generally believed, at least among scientifically minded people, that God is not required for the explanation of these facts, this is simply because evolutionary theory provides a better explanation of these same facts. Thus we see a typical indispensability argument and a typical way of resisting its conclusion—find a better explanation of the facts in question that makes no appeal to the entity in question.

Take another example. Most astronomers are convinced of the existence of so called "dark matter" to explain (among other things) certain facts about the rotation curves of spiral galaxies.[15] Again this is an indispensability argument. Anyone unconvinced of the existence of dark matter is not unconvinced of the cogency of the general form of the argument being used; it's just that they are inclined to think that there are better explanations of the facts in question.

It's not too hard to see that this form of argument is very common in both scientific and everyday usage. Indeed, in these examples, it amounts to no more than an application of inference to the best explanation. This is not to say, of course, that inference to the best explanation is completely uncontroversial. Philosophers such as Bas van Fraassen (1980) and Nancy Cartwright (1983) reject unrestricted usage of this style of inference. Typically, rejection of inference to the best explanation results in some form of anti-realism (anti-realism, or at least agnosticism, about theoretical entities in van Fraassen's case and anti-realism about scientific laws in Cartwright's case). Such people will have little sympathy for indispensability arguments. Scientific realists, on the other hand, are generally committed to inference to the best explanation, and *they* are my main target in this book.[16] Indispensability arguments about mathematics urge scientific realists to place mathematical entities in the same ontological boat as (other) theoretical entities. That is, it invites them to embrace Platonism.[17]

The use of indispensability arguments for defending mathematical realism is usually associated with Quine (1948; 1951; 1960a; 1963; 1969b; 1981b) and Putnam (1971; 1979a) but it's important to realise that the argument goes back much further. Gottlob Frege, for example, considers the difference between games such as chess and arithmetic and concludes that "it is applicability alone which elevates arithmetic from a game to the rank of a science" (Frege, 1970, p. 187). As Michael Dummett points out (1991, p. 60), Frege's appeal to the applications of arithmetic here is made

---

[15] These are graphs of radial angular speed versus mean distance from the centre of the galaxy for stars in a particular galaxy.

[16] Indeed, one of the most persuasive arguments *for* scientific realism is generally taken to appeal to inference to the best explanation. This argument is due to J. J. C. Smart (1963).

[17] I'm not claiming here that the indispensability argument for mathematical entities is simply an instance of inference to the best explanation; I'm just noting that inference to the best explanation is a kind of indispensability argument, so those who accept inference to the best explanation are at least sympathetic to this style argument.

in order to raise a problem for formalists who liken mathematics to a game in which mathematical symbols have no meaning, but are simply manipulated in accordance with certain rules. Frege asks the formalists to explain how such a game could have applications (Frege, 1970, p. 187). This is clearly a form of indispensability argument.

Kurt Gödel also appeals to what is apparently an indispensability argument in "What is Cantor's Continuum Problem?" (1947). Gödel considers reasons for adopting a new axiom of set theory and suggests that

> a probable decision about [the proposed new axiom's] truth is possible ... by studying its "success." Success here means fruitfulness in consequences, in particular in "verifiable" consequences. (Gödel, 1947, p. 477)

A little later he suggests that if the axiom in question proved to be sufficiently fruitful, then it "would have to be accepted at least in the same sense as any well-established physical theory" (Gödel, 1947, p. 477). The applications Gödel has in mind are intra-mathematical, but his argument is unmistakably an argument from applications to (probable) truth, which is enough for it to be counted as an indispensability argument.

It's no coincidence that both Frege and Gödel were mathematical realists, although neither seemed to base their realism entirely on the applications of mathematics. On the other hand, it seems they were both sensitive to the importance of the applicability of mathematics when considering mathematical truth and ontology. Frege's and Gödel's apparent endorsement of some form of indispensability argument is important in that it underlines the point that indispensability arguments for mathematical entities enjoy a wider usage than is usually realised. These arguments are not simply artefacts of the Quinean worldview. Although the form of the argument that I favour is essentially Quinean, part of my task is to disentangle this argument from the rest of the Quinean philosophical web. I will argue that while the argument does depend on a couple of Quinean doctrines (namely, confirmational holism and naturalism), it does not depend on acceptance of all of Quine's views on science and language. In particular, it does not depend on his controversial views about indeterminacy of translation and meaning.

1.2.2 The Quine/Putnam Indispensability Argument

Quine's version of the indispensability argument is to be found in many places. For instance, in "Success and Limits of Mathematization" he says:

> Ordinary interpreted scientific discourse is as irredeemably committed to abstract objects—to nations, species, numbers, functions,

sets—as it is to apples and other bodies. All these things figure as
values of the variables in our overall system of the world. The numbers and functions contribute just as genuinely to physical theory as
do hypothetical particles. (Quine, 1981b, pp. 149–150)

Here he draws attention to the fact that abstract entities, in particular
mathematical entities, are as indispensable to our scientific theories as
the theoretical entities of our best physical theories.[18] Elsewhere (Quine
(1951)) he suggests that anyone who is a realist about theoretical entities
but anti-realist about mathematical entities is guilty of holding a "double
standard." For instance, Quine points out that the position that scientific
claims, but not mathematical claims, are supported by empirical data is
untenable:

> The semblance of a difference in this respect is largely due to overem-
> phasis of departmental boundaries. For a self-contained theory which
> we can check with experience includes, in point of fact, not only its
> various theoretical hypotheses of so-called natural science but also
> such portions of logic and mathematics as it makes use of. (Quine,
> 1963, p. 367)

He is claiming here that those portions of mathematical theories that are
employed by empirical science enjoy whatever empirical support the scientific theory as a whole enjoys. (I will have more to say on this matter in
chapter 6.)

Hilary Putnam also once endorsed this argument:

> [Q]uantification over mathematical entities is indispensable for sci-
> ence, both formal and physical; therefore we should accept such
> quantification; but this commits us to accepting the existence of the
> mathematical entities in question. This type of argument stems, of
> course, from Quine, who has for years stressed both the indispensabil-
> ity of quantification over mathematical entities and the intellectual
> dishonesty of denying the existence of what one daily presupposes.
> (Putnam, 1971, p. 347)

He elaborates on this "intellectual dishonesty" in "What is Mathematical
Truth?":

---

[18] I often speak of certain entities being dispensable or indispensable to a given theory.
Strictly speaking it's not the entities themselves that are dispensable or indispensable,
but rather it's the *postulation of* or *reference to* the entities in question that may be so
described. Having said this, though, for the most part I'll continue to talk about *entities*
being dispensable or indispensable, eliminable or non-eliminable and occurring or not
occurring. I do this for stylistic reasons, but I apologise in advance to any reader who is
irritated by this.

> It is like trying to maintain that God does not exist and angels do not
> exist while maintaining at the very same time that it is an objective
> fact that God has put an angel in charge of each star and the angels
> in charge of each of a pair of binary stars were always created at the
> same time! (Putnam, 1979a, p. 74)

Both Quine and Putnam, in these passages, stress the indispensability of
mathematics to science. It thus seems reasonable to take science, or at least
whatever the goals of science are, as the purpose for which mathematical
entities are indispensable. But, as Putnam also points out (1971, p. 355), it
is doubtful that there is a single unified goal of science. (The goals include
explanation, prediction, retrodiction, and so on.) Thus, we see that we may
construct a variety of indispensability arguments, all based on the various
goals of science. As we've already seen, the explanatory indispensability
argument is one influential argument of this style, but it is important to
bear in mind that it is not the only one.

To state the Quine/Putnam indispensability argument, we need merely
replace 'ξ' in argument 1 with 'mathematical entities'. For convenience of
future reference I will state the argument here in a rather explicit form.

Argument 2 (The Quine/Putnam Indispensability Argument)

1. *We ought to have ontological commitment to all and only those enti-
    ties that are indispensable to our best scientific theories;*

2. *Mathematical entities are indispensable to our best scientific theories.*

    Therefore:

3. *We ought to have ontological commitment to mathematical entities.*

A number of questions about this argument need to be addressed. The
first is: The conclusion has normative force and clearly this normative
force originates in the first premise, but why should an argument about
ontology be normative? This question is easily answered, for I take most
questions about ontology to be really questions about what we *ought to
believe* to exist. The Quine/Putnam indispensability argument, as I've
presented it, certainly respects this view of ontology. Indeed, I take it that
indispensability arguments are essentially normative. For example, if you
try to turn the above Quine/Putnam argument into a descriptive argument,
so that the conclusion is that mathematical entities exist, you find you must
have something like "All and only those entities that are indispensable to
our best theories exist" as the crucial first premise. This premise, it seems

to me, is much more controversial than the normative one.[19] As we shall
see in the next chapter, this normativity arises in the doctrine of naturalism
on which I will have a great deal more to say.

The next question is: How are we to understand the phrase "indispensable to our best scientific theory"? In particular, what does "indispensable"
mean in this context? Much hangs on this question, and I'll need to treat
it in some detail. I'll do this in chapter 4. (In section 4.2 I give a precise account of indispensability.) In the meantime, take it to intuitively
mean "couldn't get by without" or some such. In fact, whatever sense it
is in which electrons, neutron stars, and viruses are indispensable to their
respective theories will do.[20]

The final question is: Why believe the first premise? That is, why ought
we believe in the existence of entities indispensable to our best scientific explanations? Answering this question is not easy, and an attempt to answer
it will occupy the best part of the following two chapters. Briefly, I will
argue that the crucial first premise follows from the doctrines of *naturalism*
and *holism*. Before I embark on this task, I should point out that the first
premise, as I've stated it, is a little stronger than required. In order to
gain the given conclusion all that is really required in the first premise is
the "all," not the "all and only." I include the "all and only," however,
for the sake of completeness and also to help highlight the important role
naturalism plays in questions about ontology, since it is naturalism that
counsels us to look to science and *nowhere else* for answers to ontological
questions.

As I've already made clear, I'll have more to say about naturalism and
holism in the next two chapters, but it will be useful here to outline the
argument from naturalism and holism to the first premise of argument 2.
Naturalism, for Quine at least, is the philosophical doctrine that there
is no first philosophy and the philosophical enterprise is continuous with
the scientific enterprise. What is more, science, thus construed (i.e., with
philosophy as a continuous part) is taken to be the complete story of the
world. This doctrine arises out of a deep respect for scientific methodology
and an acknowledgment of the undeniable success of this methodology as
a way of answering fundamental questions about all nature of things. As
Quine suggests, its source lies in "unregenerate realism, the robust state

---

[19] Although, arguably, once one accepts naturalism, which rules out scepticism about
science, the descriptive conclusion does follow (Resnik, 1995, pp. 171–172). For the most
part, I'll ignore this and continue to talk about what we ought to believe to exist rather
than what exists. See footnote 21 in this chapter.

[20] If you think that there is *no* sense in which electrons, neutron stars, and viruses are
indispensable to their respective theories, then the indispensability argument is unlikely
to have any appeal.

of mind of the natural scientist who has never felt any qualms beyond the negotiable uncertainties internal to science" (Quine, 1981a, p. 72). For the metaphysician this means looking to our best scientific theories to determine what exists, or, perhaps more accurately, what we ought to believe to exist. Naturalism, in short, rules out unscientific ways of determining what exists. For example, I take it that naturalism would rule out believing in the transmigration of souls for mystical reasons. It would not, however, rule out the transmigration of souls if this were required by our best scientific theories.

Naturalism, then, gives us a reason for believing in the entities in our best scientific theories and no other entities. Depending on exactly how you conceive of naturalism, it may or may not tell you whether to believe in *all* the entities of your best scientific theories. I take it that naturalism does give us *some* reason to believe in all such entities, but that this is defeasible. This is where the holism comes to the fore; in particular, confirmational holism. Confirmational holism is the view that theories are confirmed or disconfirmed as wholes. So, if a theory is *confirmed* by empirical findings, the *whole* theory is confirmed. In particular, whatever mathematics is made use of in the theory is also confirmed. Furthermore, as Putnam has stressed (1971), the same evidence that is appealed to in justifying belief in the mathematical components of the theory is appealed to in justifying the empirical portion of the theory (if indeed the empirical can be separated from the mathematical). Taking naturalism and holism together, then, we have the first premise of argument 2.

Before concluding this chapter, I would like to outline a couple of other indispensability arguments for mathematical entities. Although these arguments won't play any significant role in this work, it is, nevertheless, useful to see that the Quine/Putnam argument is not the only argument of this general form that purports to deliver mathematical realism.

1.2.3 Other Indispensability Arguments

I've already mentioned Frege's and Gödel's indispensability arguments. I've also outlined how one can construct various indispensability arguments that revolve around the various aims of science. For instance, we could easily construct an argument that relied on quantification over mathematical entities being indispensable for explanations. We could do the same for empirical predictions, retrodictions, and so on. In this section I would like to outline two slightly different forms of argument that deliver Platonism as their conclusions. The first of these is Michael Resnik's *pragmatic indispensability argument*. The other is what I will call a *semantic indispensability argument*.

Michael Resnik's (1995) pragmatic indispensability argument focuses on the purpose of "doing science" and is a response to some problems raised for the Quine/Putnam indispensability argument by Penelope Maddy and Elliott Sober. Although I won't discuss these problems here (I do so in chapters 5 and 6), one point is important in understanding Resnik's motivation. This is that he wishes to avoid the reliance on confirmational holism that the Quine/Putnam argument requires.

Resnik states the argument in two parts. The first is an argument for the conditional claim that if we are justified in drawing conclusions from and within science, then we are justified in taking mathematics used in science to be true. He states this part of the argument as follows:

> 1) In stating its laws and conducting its derivations science assumes the existence of many mathematical objects and the truth of much mathematics.
>
> 2) These assumptions are indispensable to the pursuit of science; moreover, many of the important conclusions drawn from and within science could not be drawn without taking mathematical claims to be true.
>
> 3) So we are justified in drawing conclusions from and within science only if we are justified in taking the mathematics used in science to be true. (Resnik, 1995, pp. 169–170)

He then combines the conclusion of this argument with the argument that we *are* justified in drawing conclusions from and within science since this is the only way we know of doing science and that we are justified in doing science. The conclusion, then, is that we are justified in taking whatever mathematics is used in science to be true.[21]

This argument clearly fits the mould of the scientific indispensability argument that I outlined earlier. It differs from the Quinean argument in that it doesn't rely on confirmational holism. Resnik pinpoints the difference rather nicely in the following passage:

> This argument is similar to the confirmational argument except that instead of claiming that the evidence for science (one body of statements) is also evidence for its mathematical components (another body of statements) it claims that the justification for doing science (one act) also justifies our accepting as true such mathematics as science uses (another act). (Resnik, 1995, p. 171)

---

[21] In fact, Resnik draws the additional (stronger) conclusion that mathematics is true, arguing that this follows from the weaker conclusion, since to assent to the weaker conclusion while denying the stronger invites a kind of Moore's paradox. (Moore's paradox is the paradox of asserting "*P* but I don't believe *P*.")

This argument has some rather attractive features. For instance, since it doesn't rely on confirmational holism, it doesn't require confirmation of any scientific theories in order for belief in mathematical objects to be justified. Indeed, even if *all* scientific theories were disconfirmed, we would (presumably) still need mathematics to do science, and since doing science is justified we would be justified in believing in mathematical objects. This is clearly a very powerful argument and one with which I have considerable sympathy. Although this argument will receive very little attention in what follows, it is important to see that a cogent form of argument in the general spirit of the Quine/Putnam argument can be maintained without recourse to confirmational holism.

The second argument I wish to consider in this section represents more of a departure from the Quine/Putnam argument. It does not even conform to the general pattern of a scientific indispensability argument.[22] This argument takes *semantics* as the purpose for which mathematical entities are indispensable. According to this argument, the best candidate for a uniform semantics for our everyday discourse, our scientific discourse, and our mathematical discourse is Platonism. Although the details vary, many philosophers have argued for Platonism along roughly these lines.[23]

In his famous essay "Mathematical Truth" Benacerraf pointed out:

> A theory of truth for the language we speak, argue in, theorize in, mathematize in, etc., should ... provide similar truth conditions for similar sentences. The truth conditions assigned to two sentences containing quantifiers should reflect in relatively similar ways the contribution made by the quantifiers. Any departure from a theory thus homogeneous would have to be strongly motivated to be worth considering. (Benacerraf, 1973, p. 404)

For example, consider the following sentences:

1. There's a city larger than Melbourne.

2. There's a number larger than 17.

Both of these have the logical form $(\exists x)(Fx \mathbin{\&} Lxa)$ and, what is more, both are apparently true. We would thus expect similar accounts of how each of these sentences comes to be true. (What Benacerraf is asking for is

---

[22] In fact, it is not usually taken to be an indispensability argument at all. I hope, however, that it will become apparent that this argument is indeed an indispensability argument.

[23] For example, Crispin Wright (1983), Bob Hale (1987), Steven Wagner (1996), Ed Zalta and Bernard Linsky (Linsky and Zalta (1995); Linsky (unpublished)). It might also be argued that Meinong and Frege argued for Platonism along these lines.

not just the correct distribution of truth values across the language, but a homogeneous story about why each sentence has the truth value it does.) The only account known to do this is Tarski's (or so the argument goes), and this is a *referential* semantics. This suggests that Platonism is supported by considerations of semantics.

It would certainly be a misconstrual of Benacerraf's purpose to claim that he intended this as a positive argument for Platonism. Nevertheless, such considerations do suggest a semantic route to Platonism. Steven Wagner, for one, proposes a semantic argument along these lines:

> Systematic accounts of truth or validity must apparently treat predicates and logical operators as denoting various abstracta. Thus any language in which we recognize truth or valid inference yields a Platonic universe corresponding to its expressive power. (Wagner, 1996, p. 76)

I take a general semantic indispensability argument to be something like the following:

Argument 3 (Semantic Indispensability Argument) *If apparent reference to some entity (or class of entities) ξ is indispensable to our best semantic theories of natural (and scientific) language, then we ought to believe in the existence of ξ. Abstracta are indispensable to our best semantic theory of natural (and scientific) language. Thus, we ought to believe in such abstracta.*

Although I don't wish to discuss such arguments in any detail, a few comments are warranted. Firstly, semantic indispensability arguments typically yield more abstract entities than scientific indispensability arguments. The latter only provide enough abstract entities to satisfy the needs of science, while the former provide all those and many more besides. For example, semantic considerations seem to require an abstract object for every predicate in the language in question. This highlights one of the strengths (according to some) of this style of argument—one does not have the problem of not enough abstracta.[24] On the other hand, this is seen by others to be one of the weaknesses of this style of argument—we get an extremely

---

[24] This problem seems to arise with scientific indispensability arguments—any mathematical entities that do not find applications in empirical science do not gain admission into the ontology. What is more, Bernard Linsky points out, that according to the Quine/Putnam indispensability argument, "[w]e believe in [mathematical entities] because we can't avoid it, not because we want to" (Linsky (unpublished)). He goes on to suggest that "one would like a less grudging acceptance of the abstract" (Linsky (unpublished)).

inflated ontology far too easily.[25] This leads to another weakness of this style of argument:

> The problem is that science has clearer credentials than formal semantics. Physics is acceptable beyond doubt. If it admits no nominalistic construal, then Platonism is true. Semantics, however, is not clearly science and not clearly anything else that compels belief in its ontology. (Wagner, 1996, p. 77)

Finally, it should be pointed out that it might be possible to combine the semantic and scientific indispensability arguments in such a way as to yield a plausible hybrid.[26] Nothing prevents mathematical entities from being indispensable for multiple purposes.

I will leave the discussion of general indispensability arguments there. I hope it is clear, however, that there is nothing peculiar about the Quine/Putnam argument—it is just one of many such arguments. Indispensability arguments are *not* purely an artefact of the Quinean philosophical picture. In particular, many mathematical indispensability arguments may be found in the literature. This is not to say, however, that the Quine/Putnam version of the argument doesn't rely on some substantial Quinean doctrines. As we've already seen, this argument *does* rely on holism and (Quinean) naturalism. I'll have more to say about these in the chapters ahead. Let me now outline my strategy for the remainder of the book.

1.3 The Road Ahead

As I've already suggested, I will be concerned largely with defending the Quine/Putnam version of the indispensability argument against some of its detractors.[27] I will from time to time, however, depart a little from the letter of the Quinean doctrine. I wish to make it clear that my aim is not to defend the argument exactly as Quine presents it. (Indeed, that would be difficult because there is no explicit, detailed presentation of the argument to be found anywhere in Quine's writings.) Rather, my aim is to defend an argument that derives from Quine and that I think is Quinean in spirit. I

---

[25] Sentences such as "The round square is round" seem to require the existence of a round square! To borrow a phrase from Bertrand Russell, this "has many advantages; they are the same as the advantages of theft over honest toil" (Russell, 1920, p. 71).

[26] Indeed, Wagner (1996) suggests such a position.

[27] Given that the Quine/Putnam indispensability argument is my primary interest, I'll often refer to it simply as 'the indispensability argument'. Also I will often speak of 'indispensability theory' by which I will mean the Quine/Putnam indispensability argument along with that portion of Quinean philosophy required to support this argument.

will, of course, endeavour to alert the reader when my presentation departs significantly from anything Quine is likely to accept.

In order to defend this argument, it will be necessary to defend some of the Quinean framework required to support it. In particular, I will need to defend confirmational holism and (Quinean) naturalism. While both these doctrines are important, naturalism is crucial. It turns out that a very specific form of naturalism is required to support the argument and, what is more, if another popular form of naturalism is substituted in place of the Quinean variety, we find the argument is without any force. Even worse, this other form of naturalism entails the non-existence of abstract entities! So rather than yielding a pro-Platonism conclusion, this other form of naturalism rules out many Platonist philosophies of mathematics. For these reasons it's clear that a fairly detailed defence of Quinean naturalism is in order. This I undertake in the following two chapters.

In chapter 2 I defend confirmational holism and begin the defence of naturalism. I isolate the crucial difference between the two versions of naturalism at issue: Quinean naturalism *does not* subscribe to a principle endorsed by the rival naturalism. This principle I call the Eleatic Principle and is (roughly) that we ought not believe in causally idle entities. I will devote all of chapter 3 to a discussion of this important principle, concluding that, despite the principle's intuitive plausibility, it is without justification. While not exactly a positive argument for Quinean naturalism, the discussion of chapters 2 and 3 does leave Quinean naturalism looking like the most plausible version of naturalism on the market.

In chapters 4, 5, and 6 I discuss some of the criticisms that the Quine/Putnam indispensability argument has attracted and I defend the argument against these criticisms. Chapter 4 is devoted to the influential work of Hartry Field who argues that mathematics is in fact dispensable to our best scientific theories. Furthermore, he provides an original and plausible response to the problem of explaining the applicability of mathematics. I argue, in reply, that despite his impressive efforts toward showing that mathematics is dispensable to science, Field has not yet done enough to undermine the second premise of argument 2 (page 11).

In chapter 5 I discuss some objections due to Penelope Maddy. Maddy raises problems for reconciling Quinean naturalism with confirmational holism, her main point being that naturalism authorises the legitimacy of scientific methodology and this methodology does not support confirmational holism. Chapter 6 is dedicated to defending one of the less intuitive consequences of the indispensability argument: that mathematical knowledge has an empirical character.

In the first six chapters I do not discuss at any length the details of the Platonism that the indispensability argument yields. In chapter 7 I explain why. I show that although Quine had his own favoured account of what mathematical objects are, his argument can be used to defend a surprising variety of Platonist positions. I also address the important issue of how such accounts reply to the Benacerraf challenges mentioned at the beginning of chapter 1. Finally, I look at uses of indispensability arguments outside the philosophy of mathematics and consider the fear that indispensability arguments can be used to justify too much.

[t]he naturalistic philosopher begins his reasoning within the inher-
ited world theory as a going concern. He tentatively believes all of
it, but believes also that some unidentified portions are wrong. He
tries to improve, clarify, and understand the system from within. He
is the busy sailor adrift on Neurath's boat. (Quine, 1981a, p. 72)

The aphorisms are useful, but they also mask a great deal of the sub-
tlety and complexity of Quinean naturalism. Indeed, the subtleties and
complexities of naturalism are far greater than one would expect for such a
widely held and intuitively plausible doctrine. We would thus be well served
spending a little time coming to better understand Quinean naturalism.

As I see it, there are two strands to Quinean naturalism. The first is a
normative thesis concerning how philosophy ought to approach certain fundamental questions about our knowledge of the world. The advice here is
clear: look to science (and nowhere else) for the answers. Science, although
incomplete and fallible, is taken to be the best guide to answering all such
questions. In particular, "first philosophy" is rejected. That is, Quine rejects the view that philosophy precedes science or oversees science. This
thesis has implications for the way we should answer metaphysical questions: We should determine our ontological commitments by looking to see
which entities our best scientific theories are committed to. Thus, I take it
that naturalism tells us (1) we ought to grant real status only to the entities
of our best scientific theories and (2) we ought to (provisionally) grant real
status to all the entities of our best scientific theories. For future reference
I'll call this first strand of Quinean naturalism the *no-first-philosophy thesis*
(or NFPT for short) and its application to metaphysics the *Quinean ontic
thesis*.

It is worth pointing out that the Quinean ontic thesis is distinct from
a thesis about how we determine the ontological commitments of *theories*.
According to this latter thesis, the ontological commitments of theories are
determined on the basis of the domain of quantification of the theory in
question.[4] Call this thesis *the ontological commitments of theories thesis*.
One could quite reasonably believe the ontological commitments of theories
thesis without accepting the Quinean ontic thesis. For instance, I take it
that Bas van Fraassen (1980) is such a person. He accepts that our current
physics is committed to entities such as electrons and the like, but it does
not follow that he believes that it is rational to believe in these entities in
order to believe the theory. The ontological commitments of theories thesis
is purely descriptive, whereas the Quinean ontic thesis is, as I've pointed
out, normative. From here on I shall be concerned only with the Quinean

---

[4] See Quine (1948, pp. 12–13) for details.

ontic thesis, but it is worth bearing in mind the difference, because I don't think that the ontological commitments of theories thesis rightfully belongs to the doctrine of naturalism. It is *an* answer to the question of how we determine the ontological commitments of theories, but it is not the only naturalistic way such questions can be answered.

The second strand of Quinean naturalism is a descriptive thesis concerning the subject matter and methodology of philosophy and science. Here naturalism tells us that philosophy is continuous with science and that together they aim to investigate and explain the world around us. What is more, it is supposed that this science–philosophy coalition is up to the task. That is, all phenomena are in principle explicable by science. For future reference I'll call this strand the *continuity thesis*.

Although it is instructive to distinguish the two strands of Quinean naturalism in this way, it is also important to see how intimately intertwined they are. First, there is the intriguing interplay between the two strands. NFPT tells us that we ought to believe our best scientific theories and yet, according to the continuity thesis, philosophy is part of these theories. This raises a question about priority: In the case of a conflict between philosophy and science, which gets priority? I'll have more to say on this issue in section 5.2, but for now it will suffice to say that philosophy does not occupy a privileged position. That much is clear. But it also appears, from the fact that philosophy is seen as part of the scientific enterprise, that science (in the narrow sense—i.e., excluding philosophy) occupies no privileged position either.

The second important connection between the two strands is the way in which the continuity thesis lends support to NFPT. The traditional way in which first philosophy is conceived is as an enterprise that is prior and distinct from science. Philosophical methods are seen to be a priori while those of science are a posteriori. But accepting the continuity thesis rules out such a view of the relationship between philosophy and empirical science. Once philosophy is located within the scientific enterprise, it is more difficult to endorse the view that philosophy oversees science. I'm not claiming that the continuity thesis entails NFPT, just that it gives it a certain plausibility.[5]

In the discussion so far I've glossed over the question of what constitutes our best scientific theories.[6] I'll have something to say about how we answer this question in section 4.3. What is important in the meantime is that there

---

[5] Indeed, the continuity thesis cannot entail NFPT since the former is descriptive and the latter normative.

[6] There is also the question of what constitutes a *scientific* theory as opposed to a *non-scientific* theory. I won't enter into that debate here: I'll assume that we have at least an intuitive idea of what a scientific theory is.

is room for disagreement about what our best scientific theories are.

Now let me say something about why one ought to embrace naturalism. I won't embark on a general defence of naturalism—that would be far too ambitious. Instead, I shall ask that you accept, for the sake of the discussion, some suitably broad sense of this doctrine.[7] I suggest that we accept something like the conception of naturalism that I opened section 2.1 with:

> We ought to seek only scientific accounts of reality.

(Where "scientific" is construed fairly broadly.) What I need to do now is convince you of *Quinean* naturalism. In order to do this, I'll need to identify what is distinctive about Quinean naturalism. In particular, I need to identify and justify those features of the Quinean conception of naturalism that support the crucial first premise of argument 2 on page 11.

First let me mark out the common ground. Naturalists of all ilks agree that we should look only to science when answering questions about the nature of reality. What is more, they all agree that there is at least prima facie reason to accept all the entities of our best scientific theories. That is, they all agree that there is a metaphysical component to naturalism. So they are inclined to accept the first part of the Quinean ontic thesis (the "only" part) and are inclined to, at least provisionally, accept the second part (the "all" part). (Most naturalists believe that naturalism entails scientific realism but they are inclined to be a little reluctant to embrace *all* the entities of our best scientific theories.)[8] What I take to be the distinctive feature of Quinean naturalism is the view that our best scientific theories are continuous with philosophy and are not to be overturned by first philosophy. It is this feature that blocks any first-philosophy critique of the ontological commitments of science. Consequently, it is this feature of Quinean naturalism that is of fundamental importance to the indispensability argument.

Now defences of such fundamental doctrines as naturalism are hard to come by. Typically such doctrines are justified by their fruits. So in order to defend Quinean naturalism over other versions (I've already mentioned that I won't be providing a general defence of naturalistic philosophy), I'll examine some of the consequences of the Quinean position. This examination will occupy us on and off for much of the remainder of this book (especially in the next chapter). Let me begin here by showing how Quinean

---

[7] It is worth bearing in mind that the primary targets of the indispensability argument are scientific realists disinclined to believe in mathematical entities. These scientific realists typically subscribe to some form of naturalism, so my acceptance, without argument, of a broadly naturalistic perspective is not as serious an assumption as it may first seem.

[8] For example Keith Campbell (1994) advocates "selective realism" and Quine restricts commitment to indispensable entities.

naturalism provides a nice defence against scepticism.

The sceptic might ask what justification we have for postulating physical objects from the meagre input of certain two-dimensional electromagnetic irradiation patterns on our retinas. Our theories clearly outstrip our
evidence for them, so it is the business of epistemology to give a factual
account of the relation between the two.[9] Quine points out, however, that
"the skeptical challenge springs from science itself, and that in coping with
it we are free to use scientific knowledge" (Quine, 1974, p. 3). After all,
the idea of being deceived about physical objects, for instance, depends on
science in two ways: (1) the deception consists in believing something other
than the scientific picture of the world and (2) it is science itself that informs
us that our data about the world is both incomplete and fallible. If scepticism originates within science, it is only reasonable that epistemologists
are justified in using whatever portion of science they require to combat
scepticism. From the point of view of Quine's naturalised epistemology,
there is no more secure vantage point than the vantage point of our best
scientific theories. Thus, the naturalised epistemologist "no longer dreams
of a first philosophy, firmer than science, on which science can be based; he
is out to defend science from within, against its self doubts" (Quine, 1974,
p. 3).

2.3   The Methodologies of Philosophy and Science

In this section I continue my defence of Quinean naturalism by defusing
an objection that it faces. The objection is that Quinean naturalism (in
particular the continuity thesis) fails to acknowledge an important methodological difference between science and philosophy. After all, so the objection goes, it is clear that philosophy proceeds by a priori methods, such
as thought experiments and deduction, whereas science proper proceeds by
a posteriori methods, the celebrated scientific method of hypotheses and
observation, typically involving *real* experiments and *induction*. In reply I
will rehearse Quine's argument against the possibility of a priori knowledge.
In addition to this, I wish to cast doubt on the legitimacy of characterising
philosophy as proceeding by a priori methods and science as proceeding by
a posteriori methods. Moreover, the discussion of this objection will help
elucidate certain features of Quinean naturalism—namely, its connection
to confirmational holism.

---

[9] Quine calls this relation "[t]he relation between the meager input and the torrential
output" (Quine, 1969a, p. 83).

2.3.1 The "Two Dogmas" Argument

In his famous article "Two Dogmas of Empiricism," Quine launches a two-fold attack on the analytic/synthetic distinction. Since his arguments here are well known, I won't spend too much time on them; I'll just refresh our memories with a quick review. The first part of this argument is to show that there is no non-circular definition of "analytic." For instance, he argued that we cannot define analyticity by way of the notion of synonymy. As Graham Priest (1979) points out, however, this circularity argument is not so much a condemnation of analyticity, since many important concepts can be defined only in circular terms.[10] The point here is that the circularity argument prevents a defence of analyticity by appeal to synonymy when analyticity comes under fire, because synonymy, being part of the circle, is just as much under fire as analyticity. Quine's attack proper, then, is an argument from the history of science that *no* belief can be held onto no matter what. I can do no better than to quote Quine here:

> Any statement can be held true come what may, if we make drastic enough adjustments elsewhere in the system. Even a statement very close to the periphery can be held true in the face of recalcitrant experience by pleading hallucination or by amending certain statements of the kind called logical laws. Conversely, by the same token, no statement is immune to revision. Revision even of the logical law of excluded middle has been proposed as a means of simplifying quantum mechanics; and what difference is there in principle between such a shift and the shift whereby Kepler superseded Ptolemy, or Einstein Newton, or Darwin Aristotle? (Quine, 1951, p. 43)

The main point is that the history of science has taught us that what were once considered analytic truths, such as that Pythagoras's theorem holds in our world[11] or that any massive body can be accelerated without bound, have been given up in order to cohere with new and better scientific theories. Thus, by an inductive argument from such examples, we conclude that there are no analytic truths.[12]

Putnam (1976) points out that the idea of an analytic truth as one that is confirmed no matter what is quite different from the original Kantian

---

[10] Indeed, if Quine is correct about language, this is true of *all* concepts!

[11] By this I simply mean to rule out the claim that Pythagoras's theorem holds in abstract Euclidean spaces.

[12] Perhaps the conclusion here seems a bit stronger than the argument will support, but at the very least we can conclude that even if there are analytic truths, we are notoriously bad at recognising them. We should thus give them no privileged place in science. This weaker conclusion is all that Quine really requires, and certainly all that I require in this discussion.

notion of "the predicate contained in the concept"; it is much more like the traditional notion of apriority. So if we take Quine's argument from the history of science on its own, we have an argument against the a priori/a posteriori distinction. Furthermore, the argument, thus construed, *does* stand on its own; it does not depend on the circularity argument, which has attracted some criticism since the publication of "Two Dogmas of Empiricism."[13] We see then that if the a priori/a posteriori distinction cannot be maintained, the claim that Quinean naturalism fails to recognise this distinction is misguided. Note, however, that for Quine some beliefs may be more central than others, and so may have an a priori "feel" to them but strictly speaking they are not a priori.

It is also worth noting explicitly that in the foregoing defence of the continuity thesis we have seen an important consequence of Quinean naturalism: some sort of holism about our scientific theories. The fact that we cannot distinguish between a priori and a posteriori portions of our theory and also the fact that it seems that isolated hypotheses do not enjoy empirical confirmation or disconfirmation—only bodies of hypotheses may be said to be confirmed or disconfirmed—suggests confirmational holism. While it's clear that there is a close relationship between naturalism and holism, I do not wish to take too much for granted here. I do not wish to presuppose that the confirmational holism required for the success of the indispensability argument is written into naturalism. It would be nice if it were, but I think it's safer to suppose that it is not. I will thus argue for confirmational holism separately in section 2.5. For now I'll continue my defence of Quinean naturalism against the charge that it fails to respect the methodological differences between philosophy and science.

2.3.2   How Useful Is the Distinction?

It seems that even if one accepts the argument from the preceding section, it might be objected that Quinean naturalism fails to distinguish between the quite different methodologies of philosophy and science: The former proceeds by pseudo a priori methods; that is, by relying on beliefs central to science, such as logic, whereas empirical science proceeds by clearly a posteriori methods. This objection, though, is again misguided. The history of science is littered with examples of science proceeding by apparently a priori methods. This is the domain of the theoretical scientist, who must tease out consequences of theories using deduction and thought experiments. To give but one example, Galileo's famous law that all bodies

---

[13] See, for instance, Priest (1979), Grice and Strawson (1956), and Putnam (1976) for some of these criticisms.

fall to earth with the same velocity regardless of their mass was derived, it seems, by a thought experiment, which showed that the received view from Aristotelian physics (heavier objects fall more quickly than lighter ones) was inconsistent.[14] Furthermore, this law flew in the face of empirical evidence, as stones were repeatedly observed to fall faster than leaves. The success of Galileo's law over the received view demonstrates that internal consistency is quite rightly seen as a more important feature of a scientific theory than empirical adequacy, and since determining internal consistency is the business of the theoretical scientist, pseudo a priori methods are not only part of science, they are an *important* part of science.

The converse, however, does not seem true; philosophers do not engage in empirical inquiry. I have two things to say in relation to this. The first is that this in itself doesn't seem enough to exclude philosophy from the domain of science. After all, as we have already seen, theoretical physicists don't perform experiments either, and yet no one wishes to bar them from the science club! The other relevant point here is that while philosophers don't engage in empirical inquiry themselves, they are certainly not unaware of developments in modern experimental science. For example, those philosophers working in philosophy of mind must keep a close eye on developments in experimental psychology, computer science, and neurophysiology.

Perhaps, though, there is some fundamental difference between the philosopher's thought experiments and the scientist's. Frank Jackson suggests one way someone might wish to distinguish between the two is that scientific thought experiments tell us something about the world, whereas philosophical thought experiments tell us something about the way we use our language (Jackson, 1998, p. 78). For instance, Galileo's thought experiment tells us that all objects fall with the same velocity irrespective of mass, whereas Hilary Putnam's famous "twin earth" thought experiment tells us something about the way we use the term "water."[15] This is not

---

[14] Consider two bodies, B_1 and B_2, where B_1 is heavier than B_2. If we were to tie these two bodies together with a piece of twine of sufficient strength and allow them to fall freely from the same height, Aristotelian physics would tell us: Since B_1 is heavier than B_2 we should expect B_1 to fall faster until the piece of twine becomes tight, and then B_2 will retard B_1's motion so the velocity of the system will be *slower* than if B_1 had been dropped on its own. On the other hand, the mass of the system is greater than the mass of B_1's alone and so the system's velocity should be *faster* than if B_1 had been dropped on its own.

[15] Putnam (1973) invites us to consider earth and twin earth. These two worlds are exactly alike except for the following: In the former world the occupants use the word "water" to refer to H_2O and in the latter the occupants use it to refer to some other substance XYZ, which is otherwise similar to H_2O. Putnam's (and many others') intuition is that we, occupants of earth, would not call the twin-earth substance, XYZ,

at all clear to me though. Surely all Galileo's thought experiment shows is that there is an inconsistency in Aristotelian physics, which was rectified by dropping the proposition that heavier objects fall faster than lighter ones. The contradiction *might* have been resolved by altering the way we use some of the crucial words. Indeed, it is true that Galileo's law that all bodies fall with the same velocity is false unless what we mean by "fall" is "fall *in a vacuum*." So to some extent, at least, Galileo's thought experiment does help to clarify our use of the relevant bits of language.

Perhaps a better example is Einstein's special relativity thought experiment. Much of Einstein's work in the special theory of relativity was concerned with clarifying what is *meant* by length, time, velocity, and simultaneity rather than telling us how the world is (although it clearly does the latter as well). Indeed, Einstein himself takes this view of at least part of his work in the 1905 essay on special relativity, as illustrated by the following passage:

> Thus with the help of certain imaginary physical experiments we have settled what is to be understood by synchronous stationary clocks located at different places, and have evidently obtained a definition of "simultaneous," or "synchronous," and of "time." (Einstein, 1905, p. 40)

Take for example the classical (Galilean) addition of velocities formula:

$$V_{\mathcal{G}} = v_a + v_b \tag{2.1}$$

and compare it with the relativistic formula

$$V_{\mathcal{R}} = \frac{v_a + v_b}{1 + \frac{v_a v_b}{c^2}} \tag{2.2}$$

where v_a is the velocity of some body a (moving with uniform velocity) relative to some inertial frame $\mathcal{F}$, v_b is the velocity of some other body b (also moving with uniform velocity) relative to a, $V_{\mathcal{G}}$ is the velocity of b relative to $\mathcal{F}$ in the Galilean/Newtonian theory, $V_{\mathcal{R}}$ is the velocity of b relative to $\mathcal{F}$ in the special theory of relativity, and c is the speed of light in a vacuum. It is clear that in general $V_{\mathcal{G}} \neq V_{\mathcal{R}}$ and it is well known that equation (2.2) has replaced (2.1) as the correct formula for evaluating addition of velocities.[16]

"water." Putnam's conclusion is that the meaning of "water" is not fixed entirely by the internal states of speakers.

[16] Of course (2.1) is still used for velocities small in relation to c, but it is understood that values so obtained are estimates.

It might well be argued that there is a change of meaning in some of the relevant terms (such as "velocity") for such a revision of the addition of velocities formula to occur. Similarly the replacement of the classical kinetic energy and momentum formulae in special relativity indicates changes of meanings of these terms in the new theory. The moral of all this is simply that it is not at all clear that scientific thought experiments are concerned *only* with the way the world is. They also shed light on the way we use bits of the language of the relevant theory and, in particular, which concepts are the key ones. For instance, special relativity tells us that V_R is the important concept when adding velocities, not V_G, despite the latter's intuitive appeal.

As a final attempt to maintain some sort of distinction between philosophy and science, someone might argue that Jackson's distinction between scientific thought experiments and philosophical thought experiments *can* be upheld; it's just that Einstein, for instance, was indulging in *philosophical* analysis in his 1905 essay. But surely if the distinction in question cannot be maintained by appeal to scientific and philosophical practices, then one ought to wonder whether the distinction is really picking out anything more significant than the distinction between, say, physics and chemistry. At the very least, it is clear that the boundary between philosophy and science is vague and this is enough to support the acceptance of the continuity thesis.

To sum up, then. First, if Quine is right and there really is no a priori knowledge,[17] then there can be little substance to the thought that philosophy is a priori and science a posteriori. Second, even if you disagree with Quine on this, it is not at all clear that the cleavage between the a priori and the a posteriori corresponds to any significant cleavage at all, let alone to the cleavage between philosophy and science. The fact that Quinean naturalism fails to respect such a cleavage is far from a deficiency of the position; it is one of its great strengths.

So, having dealt with what I think are the more obvious objections to Quinean naturalism, I now turn to the task of discussing its main rival.

---

[17] This may not be strictly correct. Hilary Putnam (1979b) suggests that there is at least one a priori truth, but this is of little interest since it is not the sort of proposition that is likely to play a significant role in any scientific theory. For the record, Putnam claims that the statement "Not every statement is both true and false" is true a priori since "to deny that statement would be to forfeit rationality itself" (p. 129).

2.4   The Causal Version of Naturalism

One interesting way in which someone can give an alternative account of naturalism is by giving an alternative account of what our best scientific theories are.[18] This can be done by placing some restriction on current scientific theories, such as by believing some portion of these theories and remaining instrumental about the rest.[19] This style of account is considered very seductive by many, and in this section I will consider one such account advanced by David Armstrong.

Armstrong defines naturalism "as the doctrine that reality consists of nothing but a single all-embracing spatio-temporal system" (Armstrong, 1980a, p. 149). This conception of naturalism has an important consequence (at least according to Armstrong): We should believe in only causally active entities (or perhaps, more generously, *potentially* causally active entities). I shall refer to this as the *Eleatic Principle*,[20] or causal requirement. According to Armstrong, non-spatio-temporally located entities would be incapable of acting on particulars, and so can play no explanatory role in science. He concludes that we have no rational reason to postulate them. Elsewhere he admits that the latter argument is less than conclusive, but nonetheless "gives us good reason for denying the existence of such entities" (Armstrong, 1989, p. 7). I will not discuss Armstrong's argument in any detail here (I'll have more to say about it in chapter 3, along with other justifications of the Eleatic Principle).

I've already noted the disagreement between Quine and Armstrong on the ontological status of mathematical entities. For Armstrong, nominalism follows fairly directly from the Eleatic Principle. This is in stark contrast with Quinean naturalism, which, as we've seen already, supports Platonism. Clearly the Eleatic Principle is the crucial difference. It is interesting, however, to ask after the status of this principle. If Armstrong is using the Eleatic Principle to overrule science on ontological matters—science being

[18] Clearly the alternative account of what our best scientific theories are had better not be too radical lest it cease to qualify as naturalistic. Construing astrology and literal readings of the Bible as our best scientific theories would not do.

[19] Indeed, it seems scientists themselves are instrumental about the more fanciful areas of science; that is, those which are not firmly supported by theory and experimental evidence. This instrumentalism seems to shift to realism as the area in question becomes better understood. However, I take such instrumentalism to be simply an indication that the area of theory in question *isn't* (yet) part of the best theory.

[20] It is called "the Eleatic Principle" after a passage from Plato's *Sophist* in which the Eleatic stranger suggests that causal power is the mark of being (Plato, 1935, pp. 247d–e). David Armstrong cites this passage (1978, Vol. 2, pp. 45–46) and Graham Oddie (1982) coined the phrase "the Eleatic Principle."

committed to mathematical entities and Armstrong ruling against them—
then he is guilty of practising first philosophy. Perhaps, more plausibly,
Armstrong sees the Eleatic Principle as part of our best scientific theory.

Whether the Eleatic Principle is considered part of a first philosophy or
part of our best science doesn't matter too much; it's clear that Armstrong's
naturalism is committed to a causal test of this kind. Either way, this test
will require justification and I devote the whole of the next chapter to the
important task of examining the arguments put forward for it. For now
let me join David Lewis in expressing general concerns about philosophers
who wish to interfere with science or mathematics because of commitment
to principles such as the Eleatic Principle. (Lewis is specifically speaking
of those who wish to interfere with mathematics based on the view that
there are no classes, but the general lesson is clear.) He says:

> I am moved to laughter at the thought of how *presumptuous* it would
> be to reject mathematics for philosophical reasons. How would *you*
> like the job of telling the mathematicians that they must change
> their ways, and abjure countless errors, now that *philosophy* has
> discovered that there are no classes? Can you tell them, with a
> straight face, to follow philosophical argument wherever it may lead?
> If they challenge your credentials, will you boast of philosophy's other
> great discoveries: that motion is impossible, that a Being than which
> no greater can be conceived cannot be conceived not to exist, that
> it is unthinkable that anything exists outside the mind, that time
> is unreal, that no theory has ever been made at all probable by
> evidence (but on the other hand that an empirically ideal theory
> cannot possibly be false), that it is a wide-open scientific question
> whether anyone has ever believed anything, and so on, and on, *ad
> nauseam*?
>
> Not me! (Lewis, 1991, p. 59)

Nor me!

2.5 Holism

Holism comes in many forms. Even in Quine's philosophy there are at
least two different holist theses. The first is what is usually called *semantic
holism* (although Quine calls it *moderate holism* (1981a, p. 71)) and is
usually stated, somewhat metaphorically, as the thesis that the unit of
meaning is the whole of the language. As Quine puts it:

> The idea of defining a symbol in use was ... an advance over the
> impossible term-by-term empiricism of Locke and Hume. The state-
> ment, rather than the term, came with Bentham[21] to be recognized
> as the unit accountable to an empiricist critique. But what I am now
> urging is that even in taking the statement as unit we have drawn
> our grid too finely. The unit of empirical significance is the whole of
> science. (Quine, 1951, p. 42)

Semantic holism is closely related to Quine's denial of the analytic/synthetic
distinction and his thesis of indeterminacy of translation. He argues for the
former in a few places, but most notably in "Two Dogmas of Empiricism"
(1951), while the latter is presented in *Word and Object* (1960).

   The other holist thesis found in Quine's writings is *confirmational holism*
(also commonly referred to as the Quine/Duhem thesis). As Fodor and
Lepore point out (1992, pp. 39–40), the Quine/Duhem thesis receives many
different formulations by Quine and it is not clear that all these formulations
are equivalent. For example, in *Pursuit of Truth* Quine writes:[22]

> [T]he falsity of the observation categorical[23] does not conclusively
> refute the hypothesis. What it refutes is the conjunction of sentences
> that was needed to imply the observation categorical. In order to
> retract that conjunction we do not have to retract the hypothesis in
> question; we could retract some other sentence of the conjunction
> instead. This is the important insight called *holism*. (Quine, 1992,
> pp. 13–14)

And in "Two Dogmas of Empiricism," in a much quoted passage, he suggests that "our statements about the external world face the tribunal of
sense experience not individually but only as a corporate body" (Quine,
1951, p. 41). In a similar vein in "On Mental Entities" he tells us:

> As Pierre Duhem urged, it is the system as a whole that is keyed
> to experience. It is taught by exploitation of its heterogeneous and
> sporadic links with experience, and it stands or falls, is retained or
> modified, according as it continues to serve us well or ill in the face
> of continuing experience. (Quine, 1953, p. 222)

---

[21] Interestingly, in the original version of the paper in *Philosophical Review* the ref-
erence here is to Russell. This was exchanged for Frege in the first edition of *From a
Logical Point of View* and, finally, for Bentham in the second edition of *From a Logical
Point of View* (Fodor and Lepore, 1992, p. 216).

[22] Cf. Duhem (1906, p. 187) for a similar statement of the thesis.

[23] By "observation categorical" Quine simply means a statement of the form "whenever
P, then *Q*." For example, "where there's smoke, there's fire."

In the last two of these three passages Quine emphasizes the *confirmational* aspects of holism—it's the whole body of theory that is tested, not isolated hypotheses. In the first passage he emphasizes *disconfirmational* aspects of holism—when our theory conflicts with observation, any number of alterations to the theory can be made to resolve the conflict. Despite the difference in emphasis, I take it that these theses are equivalent (or near enough). Moreover, I take it that they are all true, modulo some quibbles about how much theory is required to face the tribunal at any time.

It's somewhat ironic that Quine argues for confirmational holism (which in some form or another is a relatively uncontroversial thesis)[24] from his semantic holism, which is one of the most controversial parts of Quine's philosophy. The debate about the rejection of the analytic/synthetic distinction, in particular, is still raging half a century after the publication of "Two Dogmas of Empiricism." I don't deny that confirmational holism follows from semantic holism; it's just that there are easier, less controversial roads to confirmational holism. Since it's only confirmational holism that we require for the indispensability argument, I intend to explore these other roads and thus avoid the semantic holism debate.

Both Duhem (1906) and Lakatos (1970) have argued for confirmational holism without any (obvious) recourse to semantic considerations. They emphasize the simple yet undeniable point that there is more than one way in which a theory, faced with recalcitrant data, can be modified to conform with that data. Consequently, certain core doctrines of a theory may be held onto in the face of recalcitrant data by making suitable alterations to auxiliary hypotheses. This point is driven home by appeal to case studies from the (actual and imagined) history of science. Indeed, such is the influence of Duhem, Lakatos, and Quine on this point that now few require convincing. I will, however, present one (fictional) example, from Lakatos, to illustrate the point:

> The story is about an imaginary case of planetary misbehaviour. A physicist of the pre Einsteinian era takes Newton's mechanics and his law of gravitation, N, the accepted initial conditions, I, and calculates, with their help, the path of a newly discovered small planet, *p*. But the planet deviates from the calculated path. Does our Newtonian physicist consider that the the deviation was forbidden by Newton's theory and therefore that, once established, it refutes the theory N? No. He suggests that there must be a hitherto unknown planet *p'*, which perturbs the path of *p*. He calculates the mass, orbit, etc. of this hypothetical planet and then asks an experimental

---

[24] Of course it is not completely uncontroversial—very little in philosophy is.

astronomer to test his hypothesis. The planet p' is so small that even the biggest available telescopes cannot possibly observe it; the experimental astronomer applies for a research grant to build yet a bigger one. In three years time, the new telescope is ready. Were the unknown planet p' to be discovered, it would be hailed as new victory of Newtonian science. But it is not. Does our scientist abandon Newton's theory and his idea of the perturbing planet? No. He suggests that a cloud of cosmic dust hides the planet from us. He calculates the location and properties of this cloud and asks for a research grant to send up a satellite to test his calculations. Were the satellite's instruments (possibly new ones, based on a little-tested theory) to record the existence of the conjectural cloud, the result would be hailed as an outstanding victory for Newtonian science. But the cloud is not found. Does our scientist abandon Newton's theory, together with the idea of the perturbing planet and the idea of the cloud which hides it? No. He suggests that there is some magnetic field in that region of the universe which disturbs the instruments of the satellite. A new satellite is sent up. Were the magnetic field to be found, Newtonians would celebrate a sensational victory. But it is not. Is this regarded as a refutation of Newtonian science? No. Either yet another ingenious auxiliary hypothesis is proposed or ... the whole story is buried in a dusty volume of periodicals and the whole story never mentioned again. (Lakatos, 1970, pp. 100–101)

The story, although humourous in tone, does illustrate how much theory is employed for what might seem like straightforward scientific observations. Thus, the unit of confirmation or disconfirmation is not the single hypothesis but, rather, some substantial body of hypotheses. Moreover, a fairly good case can be made for thinking that in some instances this larger body of hypotheses is the whole of science.

Before leaving the doctrine of holism, I wish to consider one last question: Might one accept confirmational holism as stated, but reject the claim that mathematical propositions are one with the rest of science? That is, might it not be possible to pinpoint some semantic difference between the mathematical propositions employed by science and the rest, with empirical confirmation and disconfirmation reserved for the latter? Carnap (1937), with his appeal to "truth by convention," suggested precisely this. Quine, of course, denies that this can be done (1936; 1951; 1963), but the reasons for his denial would take us deep into semantic holism. For our purposes, it will suffice to note that there is no obvious way of disentangling the purely mathematical propositions from the main body of science. Our empirical theories have the so-called empirical parts intimately intertwined with the mathematical. A cursory glance at any physics book will confirm this, where one is likely to find mixed statements such as: "planets travel in elliptical orbits"; "the curvature of space-time is not zero"; "the work done by the force on the particle is given by $W = \int_a^b \mathbf{F} \cdot d\mathbf{r}$."

Thus, even if you reject Quine's semantic holism and you think that mathematical and logical language is different in kind from empirical language, you need not reject confirmational holism. In order to reject confirmational holism, you would need (at the very least) to separate the mathematical vocabulary from the empirical in all of our best scientific theories. Clearly this task is not trivial.[25] If you still feel some qualms about confirmational holism, though, you may rest assured—this doctrine will be called into question in later chapters when I discuss some of the objections to the indispensability argument. For the moment, at least, I invite you to join me in accepting confirmational holism.

2.6 The First Premise Revisited

Let me close this chapter with a summary of how confirmational holism and Quinean naturalism combine to yield the first premise of argument 2 on page 11. First, you might wonder whether holism is required for the argument. After all, (Quinean) naturalism alone delivers something very close to the crucial first premise. (More specifically, the Quinean ontic thesis is very suggestive of the required premise.) As a matter of fact, I think that the argument can be made to stand without confirmational holism: It's just that it is more secure *with* holism. The problem is that naturalism is somewhat vague about ontological commitment to the entities of our best scientific theories. It quite clearly rules out entities *not* in our best scientific theories, but there seems room for dispute about commitment to some of the entities that *are* in these theories. Holism helps to block such a move since, according to holism, it is the whole theory that is granted empirical support.

So, naturalism tells us to look to our best scientific theories for our ontological commitments. We thus have provisional support for all the entities in these theories and no support for entities not in these theories. For reasons of parsimony, however, we may wish to grant real status to only those entities that are *indispensable* to these theories. However, we are unable to pare down our ontological commitments further by appealing to some distinction based on empirical support because, according to holism,

---

[25] As we shall see, in chapter 4, Hartry Field undertakes this task for reasons not unrelated to those I've aired here.

all the entities in a confirmed theory receive such support. In short, holism blocks the withdrawal of the provisional support supplied by naturalism. And that gives us the first premise of the Quine/Putnam indispensability argument.

In the next chapter I will continue the defence of Quinean naturalism. In particular, I will demonstrate some of the serious problems that face the Eleatic Principle. (As we have seen in this chapter, this principle is the central tenet of Quinean naturalism's main rival: the causal version of naturalism.) There are three aspects to this strategy; two relevant to the task of motivating Quinean naturalism and one that's more general. First, discrediting the Eleatic Principle undermines much of the plausibility of the causal version of naturalism, leaving Quinean naturalism looking all the more attractive. Second, I will show that when one considers how the Eleatic Principle might be defended against some of the objections I raise for it, one is drawn toward a position not unlike Quinean naturalism. This again helps fortify the Quinean position. Finally, if the Eleatic Principle were tenable, it would present a quite general problem for mathematical realists, independent of the brand of naturalism subscribed to. Undermining the Eleatic Principle thus clears the way for Platonist philosophies of mathematics.

3

The Eleatic Principle

In the last chapter I identified the crucial difference between Quinean naturalism and Armstrong's causal version of naturalism. The difference, I argued, is that the latter subscribes to the Eleatic Principle, while the former does not. In this chapter I will continue the defence of Quinean naturalism. In particular, I will highlight some problems faced by the Eleatic Principle and suggest that Quinean naturalism is better equipped to deal with these difficulties.

The Eleatic Principle or causal criterion, you will recall, is a causal test that entities must pass in order to gain admission to some philosophers' ontologies. This principle justifies belief in only those entities to which causal power can be attributed, that is, to those entities that can bring about changes in the world. The idea of such a test is rather important in modern ontology, since it is neither without intuitive appeal nor without influential supporters. Its sympathisers (if not supporters) have included David Armstrong (1978, Vol. 2, p. 5), Brian Ellis (1990, p. 22), and Hartry Field (1989, p. 68), to name but a few.

Clearly this principle requires some justification. In this chapter I will look at the arguments that have been put forward for such a principle and suggest some problems for each of these. Of course in such a survey I cannot provide a decisive refutation of the principle, but I do hope to show that, despite its intuitive appeal, the Eleatic Principle's main justifications either look ad hoc or do not justify a version of the principle that delivers the intuitively correct results about some fairly uncontroversial cases. This is not an entirely negative result though. Once we look at the shortcomings of the motivations for the Eleatic Principle, a more general principle suggests itself. This more general principle looks very much like Quine's

39

thesis that we are ontologically committed to all and only the entities that are indispensable to our current best scientific theories.

Recall that I am not intending to enter into the realist/anti-realist debate in this work. I assume realism is true but that some criterion is needed to distinguish real entities from fictional ones. It should also be stressed that any criterion put forward for such a task is a *criterion of acceptance*. As Keith Campbell puts it (emphasis in original):

> This search for a criterion for the real must be understood as a search for a criterion *for us to count something as real*; it will be a principle to apply in determining whether to accord that status, given our current stage of epistemic development. There need not be, and probably cannot be, any critical mark of the real itself; the real is what is, period. (Campbell, 1994, p. 28)

Also a word or two about a precise formulation of the Eleatic Principle. Graham Oddie (1982) attacks the Eleatic Principle by systematically questioning a number of specific formulations of it. Although he does this with considerable success, I will not follow him down this path since my criticisms of the Eleatic Principle, for the most part, will not depend on any particular formulation. What I take issue with is the motivation for *any* formulation of the principle. In any case, it may be useful to specify a particular version, just by way of example. I suggest the following is as good as any (although I stress that nothing hangs on this particular statement of the principle):[1]

Principle 1 (The Eleatic Principle) *An entity is to be counted as real if and only if it is capable of participating in causal processes.*

In one direction principle 1 is reasonably uncontroversial. Most realists agree that causal activity is a *sufficient* condition for an entity to be counted as real.[2] (It is more controversial that entities *capable* of participating in causal processes ought to be counted as real [as Principle 1 asserts], for it might be argued that Pegasus would pass such a test.) The important question, for our purposes, is whether causal activity is a *necessary* condition for an entity to be counted as real. In what follows I will argue that it is not.

---

[1] At this stage I will remain vague about what participation in a causal process amounts to. I will discuss this matter further in section 3.4.

[2] Ian Hacking (1983) argues for this claim by applying his interventionist test: Those entities that can be manipulated as tools in scientific investigations, as opposed to those that are merely tested for, are to be granted real status.

3.1 The Inductive Argument

The first motivation for a causal criterion I will consider is an inductive argument from uncontroversial cases of real entities. We start by noting that there are some fairly widely held intuitions (among realists at least) about roughly where the demarcation between the real and the instrumental should be. It should include physical objects, including theoretical entities, perhaps fields and hence waves as disturbances in these fields, among the real entities, but should not include (concrete) possible worlds[3] and frictionless planes. We thus see an initial motivation for the causal criterion: All the things that we intuitively think of as real are the sorts of things that participate in causal processes (in this world at least), whereas those that we intuitively think of as unreal do not participate in such processes.

Thus motivated, the Eleatic Principle is an inductive hypothesis about the way the world is. We look at the things in the world that are uncontroversially real, such as tables and chairs, and notice that they are all causally active. Then, by induction, we conclude that all real entities are causally active. At first glance a causal criterion thus motivated looks as if it is purely descriptive—it lacks the normative force that a criterion of acceptance, such as principle 1, ought to have. This defect, however, is easily rectified by appeal to naturalism (of almost any variety), which does make substantial normative claims about what we ought to believe. For example, if all evidence suggested that all real entities are causally active (a purely descriptive claim), then naturalism commands us to *believe* that all real entities are causally active (the corresponding normative claim). It is important to bear in mind that something like naturalism is required to get from purely descriptive theses to normative ones. In any case, since we are presupposing naturalism of some form or other, I will not dwell upon the descriptive–normative distinction.

There is a more substantive objection to this motivation though, which is that there are many other properties that the uncontroversially real entities share and that the uncontroversially unreal entities lack. All the uncontroversially real entities are spatio-temporally located, for instance. Indeed, there is argument on this very issue between protagonists of a strictly causal criterion, such as Brian Ellis, and the likes of Hartry Field, who require causal efficacy *or* spatio-temporal location. The reality of space-time points hangs crucially on whether it's causal efficacy or spatio-temporal location that is the important property. Similarly, we could opt for the property of having a positive rest mass as the mark of the real and

---

[3] Even David Lewis (1986b, p. 135) grants that modal realism is counterintuitive, which is all I'm claiming here.

again the demarcation would be different.

Worse still, it seems that such an inductive argument is going to depend on what our set of uncontroversially real entities is taken to be. For instance, if we decide to be fairly cautious about selecting the members of this set, and only admit medium-sized solid objects, we might conclude that all real entities are coloured. In light of these considerations, how do we come to decide to pin our hopes on causal efficacy and not on other properties?

One possible answer to this question is to argue that it is by virtue of an entity's causal efficacy that we have epistemic access to it, whereas other properties don't force themselves on us like this.[4] In any case, it seems fairly natural to suppose that we have epistemic access to any entity that we are to count as real. I am thus suggesting that it looks as though it is epistemic access that is in fact the prime motivation for the Eleatic Principle and not the inductive argument at all. At the very least, the inductive argument needs supplementing and this epistemic argument seems to fit the bill.

3.2 The Epistemic Argument

The epistemic considerations are perhaps the most common motivation for the Eleatic Principle. The argument is simply that even if there were causally idle entities, we would have no reason to believe in them, since their causal idleness would ensure that they didn't causally interact with us.[5]

A little consideration, however, reveals that this motivation is also somewhat thin, since the Eleatic Principle, depending on exactly how we formulate it, will require either that entities are causally active or that they are causally active with humans. The latter alternative, I suggest, looks far too anthropocentric to warrant serious consideration, for surely we ought to believe in stars and planets outside our own light cone[6] even though they are not causally interactive with us. To deny the existence of such entities is to effectively believe that the earth is the centre of the universe. This leaves only the "causally active (not necessarily with us)" formulation. On this reading, though, the epistemological motivation is lost altogether, for there may be many perfectly legitimate real entities involved in causal

---

[4] Recall that we seek "a criterion for us to count something as real" (Campbell, 1994, p. 28), so we may well admit that there are other properties that all the uncontroversially real entities share, but if we don't (or can't) have epistemic access to these entities by virtue of these other properties, then we can hardly use such properties as criteria of existence.

[5] This argument is, of course, due to Paul Benacerraf (1973).

[6] That part of the universe close enough to us so that there has been sufficient time since the Big Bang for light to reach us from it.

networks, but because they are not causally interactive with us, they suffer the same epistemic worries as causally idle entities. Again stars, planets, and so on outside our light cone are the prime examples here. That is, the set of entities whose existence may be motivated by this epistemic concern form a proper subset of the set of causally active entities.

In fact, the Eleatic Principle motivated by epistemic concerns seems to suffer all the same worries that the causal theory of knowledge suffers.[7] In particular, it seems that we have no reason to believe in future objects (whether causally active or not), and even universal empirical facts obtained by induction are likely to be problematic. Colin Cheyne (1998), who defends an epistemically motivated causal criterion, suggests the rather promising move to *kinds* of entities in order to overcome some of these problems. He suggests the following principle:[8]

Principle 2 *We cannot know that F's exist unless our belief in their existence is caused by at least one event in which an F participates.*

He argues for this principle based mainly on evidence from scientific practice—what it takes to convince scientists of the existence of a new type of entity. For example, he cites the discovery of the planet Neptune as evidence for principle 2. The existence of Neptune was predicted in 1845–6 jointly by Leverrier and Adams based on Newtonian gravitational theory and anomalies in the orbit of Uranus. It seems that the scientists of the time were unwilling to acknowledge the existence of Neptune until Galle first directly observed the planet in 1846. Cheyne claims that the moral to be drawn from such episodes in the history of science is "interacting is knowing" (1998, p. 40).

First note that this example is not entirely appropriate, since we certainly had causal contact with Neptune prior to Galle's visual contact, as Cheyne admits—we had indirect causal contact via its disturbance on the orbit of Uranus. Furthermore, a new planet may not qualify as a new kind of entity since it is of the same kind (namely, planet) as the earth.[9] In any case, leaving these points aside, there is another moral to be drawn from this and the other of Cheyne's examples. The moral I draw is "don't settle

---

[7] See Steiner (1975) for some of these.

[8] Cheyne offers this principle as a "first attempt" (p. 38) and later refines it to meet some objections. The objections I have to the principle, though, are not deflected by his later modifications, so I shall be content to deal with his first statement of the principle. See also Beall (2001) for related criticisms of Cheyne's principle.

[9] This point illustrates a difficulty with the move to kinds of entities—the difficulty of deciding whether a new entity is of a different kind to other entities already accepted. I will not pursue this point though, because I think Cheyne's approach has other, more serious problems.

for indirect evidence if you can do better." Clearly in the Neptune example-ple direct visual evidence was better than orbital disturbances of Uranus, and scientists sought this better evidence because it was possible. Contrast this with the announcement by Wolszczan and Frail in 1992 of one of the first discoveries of planets outside our own solar system. These planets were detected because of the effects they were having on a nearby pulsar, PSR1257 + 12. Here visual contact was out of the question due to their distance from earth, and yet it seems there was no reservation on behalf of the discoverers about making full-blooded existence claims:

> [W]e demonstrate that ... the pulsar is orbited by two or more planet-sized bodies. The planets detected so far have masses of at least 2.8 $M_\oplus$ and 3.4 $M_\oplus$, where $M_\oplus$ is the mass of the Earth. Their respective distances from the pulsar are .47AU and .36AU, and they move in almost circular orbits with periods of 98.2 and 66.6 days. (Wolszczan and Frail, 1992, pp. 145–147)

Perhaps a better example is that of the discovery of the element germanium. In 1871 there had been no (known) causal contact with this element, and, in fact, causal contact wouldn't come until Winckler isolated the metal in 1887. However, because of the "gap" in Mendeleeff's periodic table corresponding to the position of germanium, much was known of its chemical behaviour. Cheyne claims that

> [i]f [Mendeleeff] believed, prior to 1887, in the existence of germanium, that belief, although true, would not count as knowledge. It could only be a lucky guess, unless it was actually caused, in an appropriate way, by events in which germanium atoms participated. (Cheyne, 1998, p. 36)

Even if I were to agree that if Mendeleeff believed in the existence of germanium prior to 1887, it would not count as knowledge, it seems extremely harsh to call such a belief "a lucky guess." After all, it's not as though he would have had *no* reason to believe that germanium existed, for there was surely reason to believe that something ought to fill the relevant gap in the periodic table. (Perhaps because of some argument from past predictive success of the table or some appeal to symmetry.) It's not a lucky guess in the same sense that a lottery winner guesses the winning numbers. I claim that, at the very least, Mendeleeff would have had *reason to believe* in germanium prior to 1887. This is all we are interested in here. If you accept this claim, then this example, while perhaps not a counterexample to the causal theory of knowledge, looks like a counterexample to an epistemically motivated Eleatic Principle (such as one motivated by principle 2), since Mendeleeff had justified belief in a novel substance without the causal contact that principle 2 requires.[10]

It seems clear that appeal to the causal theory of knowledge (which is, after all, what is at the bottom of the epistemic justification), and all its notorious difficulties, is not the right approach for a justification of a causal restriction on ontological commitment. For one thing, an Eleatic Principle thus justified leaves out too many uncontroversially real entities (stars and planets outside our light cone), and second, even if one were to accept the causal theory of knowledge, there is no reason to insist that such acceptance implies that causal contact is necessary for *justified belief*, as the last example illustrates.[11] Furthermore, Cheyne's move to *kinds* of entities does not save the Eleatic Principle from these objections.[12]

3.3   The Argument from Causal Explanation

In this and the next section I will address what I take to be the most important argument for the Eleatic Principle. This argument, in its most compelling form at least, is due to David Armstrong. Armstrong has defended the Eleatic Principle in various places. For example, he proposes the following dilemma. "Are these [abstract] entities capable of *acting upon particulars*, or are they not," he asks (1978, Vol. 1, p. 128). He then raises difficulties for the first horn of the dilemma, since typically causation involves one change bringing about another, and yet here we have unchanging abstract entities presumably bringing about changes by "some sort of steady, unchanging, pressure" (1978, Vol. 1, p. 129). He concludes that "[s]uch a notion is perhaps barely possible, but it is impossible to see how such alleged causal operation could ever be identified" (1978, Vol. 1, p. 129). The other horn of the dilemma is simply that "Occam's razor ... enjoins us not to postulate them" presumably because causally idle entities have no role to play in science (1978, Vol. 1, p. 130). As Graham Oddie puts it (on behalf of Armstrong):

---

[10] Of course, germanium is *capable* of participating in causal processes, so the Eleatic Principle as I set it out in principle 1 would not rule out belief in germanium prior to 1887. This just serves to highlight the gulf between the Eleatic Principle and an epistemic motivation for it.

[11] It might even be reasonable to argue that many of our basic justified beliefs require causal contact, but this does not mean that inferential beliefs require causal contact. For example, if I am justified in believing P (because I have had causal contact with the truthmaker of P, say) and I am justified in believing that P implies Q, then surely I am justified in believing Q, whether or not I have causal contact with Q's truthmaker. I am indebted to Peter Forrest and John Bigelow for this point.

[12] In fairness to Cheyne, though, he is interested in a causal criterion of *existence*, whereas I am interested in a causal criterion of *justified belief*.

They are 'causally idle' and hence 'idle'. Respectable entities work for
their living, and there is no social security in Armstrong's universe.
(Oddie, 1982, pp. 285–286)

Armstrong has more to say about this second horn of the dilemma:

To postulate entities which lie beyond our world of space and time is,
in general, to make a speculative, uncertain, postulation. The postulation may perhaps be defended if it can be presented as *explaining*
some or all of the spatio-temporal phenomena. But if the entities
postulated lie beyond our world, and in addition have no causal or
nomic connections with it, then the postulation has no explanatory
value. Hence (a further step of course) we ought to deny the existence
of such entities. (Armstrong, 1989, pp. 7–8)

Here Armstrong explicitly cites (and emphasises) the role entities play in
explanations as the key to justifying the Eleatic Principle.[13] In a way this
is not at all surprising, since explanation often plays a key role in justifying
scientific realism.[14] It would seem only fitting that explanation should also
provide some guide as to the extent of that realism.

While I agree with Armstrong's rejection of the atypical causal action
of the first horn of the dilemma, I don't think that the postulation of
causally idle entities has no explanatory value. If this were true, then all
genuine explanations in science would have to make essential reference to
causally active entities. That is, all scientific explanations would be fully
causal explanations, but this is not the case.[15] There are many instances
of causally idle entities playing important explanatory roles in scientific
theories and I will give a few examples of such cases.

Before I proceed to the examples of explanations in science featuring
non-causal entities, I should mention that I do not wish to presuppose
any particular model of explanation,[16] nor, for that matter, any particular
model of causation. For obvious reasons I wish to be as broad-minded as

---

[13] He also explicitly appeals to explanation in Armstrong (1980a, pp. 154–155).

[14] For instance, J. J. C. Smart's (1963, p. 39) cosmic coincidence argument which, very
crudely, is that the best explanation for the world behaving *as if* there were theoretical
entities, is that the entities in question actually exist (if not it would be a remarkable
coincidence).

[15] In the discussion following a presentation of material from this chapter, David Armstrong denied that his argument for the Eleatic Principle relies on all explanation being
causal (despite the textual evidence I present here). Be that as it may, the argument I
present in this section, whether or not it is the argument Armstrong intended, has considerable plausibility and is worthy of careful attention. For convenience I will continue
to attribute the argument (as I read it) to Armstrong.

[16] Although I am inclined toward Philip Kitcher's (1981) account of explanation as
unification.

possible about both causation and explanation. I will assume only that an explanation must be enlightening—it must make the phenomena being explained *less mysterious*. If it does not fulfil this minimal requirement, I suggest that it has no right to be called "an explanation" at all. As for the nature of causation, here I need only appeal to some widely held intuitions about what sorts of entities are taken to be causally idle (for example, geometric entities and functions). Beyond this, I leave the nature of causation completely open.

I should also explain why I won't be appealing to a couple of obvious examples of non-causal explanations. The first is mathematical explanations of mathematical facts. For instance, when seeking an explanation of Gauss's *Theorema Egregium*[17] one does not find a causal one. Perhaps this goes without saying. Anyway, I will not be discussing such examples because, although they are undoubtedly non-causal explanations, they are not explanations of *events*, and it is for these that it is sometimes claimed that no non-causal explanations may be found.[18]

The second example of non-causal explanations that I won't be considering comprises the Einstein-Podolsky-Rosen cases in quantum mechanics. It might seem a little odd to leave these aside, since many would argue that these offer some of the best candidates for non-causal explanations. My reason for leaving these cases aside, however, is that I think they are very difficult to interpret. It is not clear whether the explanations are non-causal, or as some suggest, reverse-causal.[19] Such cases cast significant doubt on traditional notions of causal explanations. The examples I present, however, I take to be less controversial and hence more damaging to the view that all explanations are causal.

3.3.1 The Bending of Light

We are told that the path of a beam of light is bent in the vicinity of a massive object; the more massive the object, the greater the bending. This result was first observed in 1919 by comparing the position of a star when its light passed near the sun (during a solar eclipse) with its usual position. What is the explanation for this bending?

The preferred explanation, offered by general relativity, is geometric. It's not that something *causes* the light to deviate from its usual path; it's

---

[17] This remarkable theorem states that the Gaussian curvature of a surface is intrinsic (McCleary, 1994, p. 148).

[18] David Lewis (1986a, p. 221), for one, claims that there are no non-causal explanations of (particular) events.

[19] See, for example, Price (1996; 1999) and Dowe (1997) for interesting discussions of what amount to reverse-causal accounts of the Einstein-Podolsky-Rosen cases.

simply that light travels along space-time geodesics[20] and that the curvature of space-time is greater around massive objects. Typically the defender of causal explanations will point out that it is the mass of the object that *causes* the curvature of space-time, and so there *is* an underlying causal explanation after all. There are two fairly serious problems with this reply though. The first is the difficulty of spelling out, in a causally acceptably way, how it is that mass brings about the curvature of space-time. After all, it can't be that there is an exchange of energy or momentum between the object and space-time, as some accounts of causation require. As I have already said, I wish to remain noncommittal with respect to the details of causation, but it seems that any account that permits mass to *cause* the curvature of space-time is unintuitive to say the least.

There is undoubtedly covariance between mass and curvature, but all covariance need not be cashed out in terms of causation.[21] For example, the angle sum of a triangle covaries with the shape of the space in which it is embedded, but one is not inclined to say that the angle sum of a triangle *causes* the shape of the relevant space. It seems to me that the case of mass and the shape of space-time is similar to this. Another way of looking at this difficulty is by asking the question: Why is it not the case that the curvature of space-time causes the mass? Simple covariance doesn't guarantee that one of the factors causes the other.

The second problem for this line of argument is that there are solutions to the Einstein equation for empty space-times in which the curvature of space-time is not identically zero. These are the non-Minkowski vacuum solutions (Peat, 1992, p. 17).[22] Thus, we see that, at the very least, mass cannot be the *only* cause of curvature. What then is causing the curvature in the vacuum solutions case? There is nothing *to* cause it! It simply looks as though the curvature is uncaused. Why then insist on a causal explanation of the curvature in the universes *with* mass? I suggest that

---

[20] In fact, it's probably better to say (tenselessly) that light *lies* along space-time geodesics.

[21] Physicists, I'm told, are more inclined to think of curvature as a *manifestation* of mass.

[22] The situation is somewhat complicated though, since the positive mass theorem of general relativity states, in effect, that such solutions must have a singularity, without which the space-time would be flat. This is assuming the ADM (after R. Arnowitt, S. Deser, and C. W. Misner) conception of mass. (This is a *global* conception of mass.) Adopting the stress-energy tensor conception of mass (which is a *local* conception of mass), however, non-singular, non-Minkowski, vacuum solutions are possible. For example, the analytic extension of the Schwarzchild metric (see d'Inverno (1992, pp. 219–221)) through the singularity has non-zero ADM mass but the stress-energy mass is everywhere zero. What is more, this space-time is non-singular and non-flat. I am indebted to Robert Bartnik and Matthew Spillane for their help with this point.

there is no reason at all and we ought to simply accept the geometric explanation for the bending of light.

3.3.2 Antipodal Weather Patterns

We discover that at some time t_0 there are two antipodal points p_1 and p_2 on the earth's surface with exactly the same temperature and barometric pressure. What is the explanation for this coincidence?

Notice that there are really two coincidences to be explained here: (1) Why are there *any* such antipodal points? and (2) Why p_1 and p_2 in particular? The first explanation I will offer is a causal explanation (i.e., featuring only causally active entities) and it addresses the second question. This explanation, presumably, will trace the causal history of the current weather patterns, to arbitrary fine detail if necessary, to account for the weather patterns at p_1 and p_2. In particular, the temperature and pressure readings at p_1 and p_2 at time t_0 will be accounted for. Notice that an explanation such as this does not explain why p_1 and p_2 have the *same* temperature and barometric pressure, just why each has the particular temperature and pressure that they have, and that these *happen* to be the same. Thus, an important part of the original phenomenon is left unexplained.

This case looks similar to that of explaining why there were 11 fatalities on New South Wales roads over the 1995 Easter break. The causal story will give the causal history of each fatality but will not explain why, in particular, there were 11 fatalities. This does not seem like such a deficiency in the road fatalities case, since it seems as though there is nothing (significant) left to be explained above and beyond what the causal story tells us. The case of the antipodal weather conditions, though, is entirely different.

The difference is due to a theorem of algebraic topology that states that for any time t there are antipodal points on the surface of the earth that simultaneously have the same temperature and barometric pressure.[23] This theorem, or more correctly the proof of this theorem, provides the missing part of the causal explanation. It guarantees that there will be two such antipodal points at any time, and, furthermore, the explanation makes explicit appeal to non-causal entities such as continuous functions and spheres.

---

[23] This theorem is a corollary of the Borsuk-Ulam theorem, combined with some minor structural assumptions (i.e., that the earth is topologically equivalent to a sphere and that temperature and pressure change continuously across its surface) (Kosniowski, 1980, pp. 157–159).

Notice, though, that this explanation also has its limitations—it does not explain why it is p_1 and p_2 in particular that have the same temperature and pressure. So we see that for a complete explanation of the phenomenon in this example, we require both causal and non-causal elements in the explanation.

3.3.3   The FitzGerald-Lorentz Contraction

The special theory of relativity tells us, amongst other things, that a body in motion, relative to some inertial reference frame $\mathcal{F}$, suffers a FitzGerald-Lorentz contraction. This is a reduction in the length of the body in the direction of motion, as measured by an observer stationary with respect to $\mathcal{F}$. What is the explanation for this contraction?

Minkowski's great contribution to relativity was in offering an elegant explanation for the Lorentz transformations (including the FitzGerald-Lorentz contraction). This explanation appeals to the now familiar concept of space-time, that is, a three-plus-one-dimensional manifold, which consists of three spatial dimensions and one temporal dimension. Minkowski realised that one of the key assumptions of special relativity, the constancy of the speed of light, could be formalised as the satisfaction of the equation:

$$(\Delta x_1)^2 + (\Delta x_2)^2 + (\Delta x_3)^2 - c^2(\Delta t)^2 = 0 \tag{3.1}$$

in any inertial frame. Here x_1, x_2, and x_3 are the spatial coordinates, t is the temporal coordinate, and c is a constant (the speed of light in a vacuum). Minkowski then introduces the imaginary time coordinate

$$x_4 = ict$$

where as usual $i = \sqrt{-1}$. So (3.1) becomes:

$$(\Delta x_1)^2 + (\Delta x_2)^2 + (\Delta x_3)^2 + (\Delta x_4)^2 = 0 \tag{3.2}$$

and (3.2) will be satisfied in every inertial frame if the quantity

$$\sigma^2 = (\Delta x_1)^2 + (\Delta x_2)^2 + (\Delta x_3)^2 + (\Delta x_4)^2 \tag{3.3}$$

is invariant under Lorentz transformation. This, says Einstein, "shows that the Lorentz transformation so defined is identical with the translational and rotational transformations of Euclidean geometry, if we disregard the number of dimensions and the relations of reality" (Einstein, 1967, p. 31). That is, the FitzGerald-Lorentz contraction is nothing more mysterious than the apparent shortening of an object in one dimension when a new set of axes are chosen, inclined at some angle to the old. This latter thesis is the invariance of length under translation and rotation and is expressed mathematically as the invariance of the quantity

$$s^2 = (\Delta x_1)^2 + (\Delta x_2)^2 + (\Delta x_3)^2 \tag{3.4}$$

under linear transformations with determinate $|1|$ (i.e., the transformations are neither contractions nor expansions).

The explanation for the FitzGerald-Lorentz contraction is seen very clearly when one realises that the quantity s^2 in equation (3.4) is not invariant under Lorentz transformation in Minkowski space (although it *is* under rotation and translation in $\mathbb{R}^3$, as we have seen). The relevant invariant in Minkowski space is σ^2, as given by equation (3.3). I also stress the obvious here: this is a purely geometric explanation of the contraction, featuring such non-causal entities as the Minkowski metric and other geometric properties of Minkowski space.[24]

3.4   Causal Relevance

In this section I investigate another reply that supporters of the causal criterion are liable to make. This is to deny the causal idleness of the entities in examples such as those presented in the last section. One plausible way this can be done is to claim that the entities in the explanation are *causally relevant* but not *causally efficacious*. Frank Jackson and Philip Pettit (1990) give a good account of this approach. Although Jackson and Pettit don't specifically put the notion of causal relevance to work salvaging the causal criterion, nonetheless, their program could be used for this purpose.

Consider a case of trying to fit a square peg of side length ℓ into a round hole of diameter ℓ. Clearly it will not go. The first reason is non-causal: because of the squareness of the peg (and the roundness of the hole). The second is causal: the resistance offered by the overlapping portion of the peg. Furthermore, it seems that someone in possession of the squareness explanation knows more than someone who knows only the overlapping explanation. Jackson and Pettit suggest, and I agree with them here, that although the abstract property of squareness did not *cause* the overlapping, nor did it combine with the overlapping to produce the blocking, it is certainly true that the squareness was efficacious only if the overlapping was. They conclude that the abstract property of squareness is not causally efficacious (at least in this example). There is a sense, though, in which it

---

[24] I am indebted to Jack Smart for drawing my attention to this examples such as this in both discussion and in his article (1990).

is not causally irrelevant either. It is not irrelevant in the way in which, say, the colour of the peg is. On this, Jackson and Pettit have the following to say:

> Although not efficacious itself, the abstract property was such that its realization ensured that there was an efficacious property in the offing. (Jackson and Pettit, 1990, p. 116)

That is, the property of squareness *programs* for the efficacious property of overlapping portions.

While I think there is much to be said for the causal relevance approach, in the end it won't save the causal criterion, for as I see it there are two serious difficulties facing this approach. First, I don't think that this defence will work for all explanations making use of non-causal entities. It will work only for those in which a fully causal explanation (i.e., one in which *all* the entities in question are causally efficacious) is on offer as well as the non-causal one, or where there are non-causal elements in a largely causal explanation. Thus, this strategy won't work for the FitzGerald-Lorentz contraction case where only one explanation is on offer and it is non-causal. Second, although this strategy enables supporters of the causal criterion to classify many apparently non-causal entities as causal, this is done at a fairly high price: significant blurring of the distinction between the causal and the non-causal. This blurring, if serious enough, is just the sort of thing that antagonists of the causal criterion would welcome. After all, if the property of squareness can enter into causal explanations, albeit in a subsidiary role (i.e., as causally relevant rather than causally efficacious), it seems that the causal requirement lets in too much. I am more inclined to admit that causally idle entities can have explanatory power than to fiddle with the definition of "causal" in this way.

One final move is left open to the supporter of the claim that only causally active entities can have explanatory power, and this is to argue that the geometry of space-time, for instance, while not being causally efficacious, nor programming for causally efficacious properties, may predetermine the range of possibilities. Space-time is thus seen as a *structuring cause* in Dretske's language. This move will allow the supporter of the causal criterion to classify the remaining recalcitrant explanations I've presented as fully causal explanations. But now I think that the difference between such a position and my own is entirely terminological. After all, what is the difference between holding (a) that there are causally idle entities with explanatory power and (b) that only causally active entities have explanatory power but that some of those entities might be structures that are not directly involved in causal chains? I suggest that whether one classifies such structures as causal or not, the important point is the recognition of the importance of such structures in scientific explanations.

Where does this leave us then? Either there are causally idle entities with explanatory power, such as the geometry of space-time, or only causally active entities have explanatory power but they may include structural elements such as the geometry of space-time and programming properties such as continuous temperature distribution functions. Clearly it is the former conclusion I have been arguing for, but the latter will do as well. If the causal criterion is motivated by a notion of causally active entity that must include geometric properties, continuous functions, and the like, then it is ill equipped to make the demarcation required of it. Geometric properties and mathematical entities are just the sorts of entities the causal criterion is usually thought to eliminate. Perhaps this is not a terribly damaging argument against the causal criterion. After all, you could just bite the bullet and accept that the causal criterion does not rule out mathematical and geometric properties as is commonly thought. But surely mathematical and geometric entities are paradigm cases of non-causal entities. It looks as though the causal criterion is preserved in name only.

3.5 Rejecting Inference to the Best Explanation

In the previous two sections I discussed, at some length, the motivation for the Eleatic Principle that rested ultimately on the claim that only causally active entities can have explanatory power. It might be useful at this stage to make explicit one further assumption that defenders of the Eleatic Principle have thus far accepted. They have all accepted the view that we have ontological commitment to the entities in our best scientific explanations. That is, the defenders of the Eleatic Principle we've met so far accept inference to the best explanation. But now another defence of the Eleatic Principle presents itself. This defence is to accept that there are non-causal entities with explanatory power, but to reject inference to the best explanation in its most general form. This position has been defended by Nancy Cartwright (1983). Cartwright argues for inference to the most likely cause instead of the more general inference to the best explanation. Brian Ellis argues for a similar position. Ellis accepts that science makes extensive use of non-causal explanation, but he argues that only fully causal explanations carry ontological commitment.[25] If some restriction on inference

---

[25] Of course there are other issues on which Cartwright and Ellis have substantial disagreement. For instance, Cartwright is anti-realist about (most) of our best scientific

to the best explanation to causal explanations can be sustained, then the
Eleatic Principle is justified trivially. I consider Cartwright's and Ellis's
arguments for such a restriction in this section.

3.5.1   Ellis's Argument

Ellis is a scientific realist and, like many other realists, is so largely because
of Smart's cosmic coincidence argument (which I mentioned in section 3.3).
There is one difference, though. Ellis does not accept inference to the best
explanation as Smart does. Ellis claims that "[o]ntological commitment can
derive only from causal process explanations" (1990, p. 22). The latter is
enough for a restricted version of Smart's argument to go through. The
resulting realism is restricted to causally active entities:

> The ontology does not admit abstract entities like propositions and
> sets, unless these can somehow be reduced to entities of other kinds.
> For such entities have no causes or effects, have no location in space
> or time, and cannot influence any causal processes. It is argued that
> while such entities may have a role in model theoretic explanations,
> acceptance of such explanations carries no ontological commitments;
> only the acceptance of causal explanations carries any such commit-
> ment to the entities involved. The entities occurring in our model
> theories should generally be regarded as fictions. (Ellis, 1990, p. 5)

His reason for restricting inference to the best explanation in this way is
apparent once we distinguish between two quite different types of scientific
explanation. The first is the causal explanation, which, on Ellis's account of
causation, will typically involve a story about exchanges of energy between
physical entities. The second type of explanation is what Ellis calls *model
theoretic explanations*. These typically idealise away from real situations
and they are used as backgrounds for causal explanations. For example,
Newton's first law provides the background for a causal explanation of why
some moving object comes to rest. These model theoretic explanations
typically feature such obviously fictional entities as frictionless planes, non-
turbulent, laminar flow and inertial reference frames, so we should not
accord real existence to the entities that feature in such explanations.

While I agree that this argument presents good reason to be suspicious
of entities in such model theoretic explanations, it says nothing of abstract
entities that feature in causal explanations. For example, in a fully causal
account of a billiard ball collision (i.e., with frictional forces, etc.), we will

---

theories, whereas Ellis is not.

find reference to vectors.[26] Ellis acknowledges as much in the following passage:

> The main argument for realism about theoretical entities is also, apparently, an argument for the existence of forces, fields, numbers, sets, spatio-temporal relationships, possible worlds, and many other kinds of things. (Ellis, 1990, pp. 60–61)

But he has another reason for insisting that abstract entities have no real existence:

> The basic reason for resisting abstract particulars is that the world we can know about would be the same whether or not they existed. (Ellis, 1990, p. 79)

The key phrase here is "the world we can *know* about." Clearly some causal theory of knowledge is alluded to here, for otherwise the statement is patently false.[27] So in the end Ellis's restriction of the application of inference to the best explanation to causal process explanations will not provide a justification for the Eleatic Principle (by his own admission—see the second last quotation), so we are back to the epistemic justification that I discussed and dismissed in section 3.2.

3.5.2 Cartwright's Argument

Nancy Cartwright is also a realist of sorts. She is a realist about theoretical entities but not about scientific theories. She sums up her view rather nicely in the following passage:

> I believe in theoretical entities. But not in theoretical laws. Often when I have tried to explain my views on theoretical laws, I have met with a standard realist response: 'How *could* a law explain if it weren't true?' Van Fraassen and Duhem teach us to retort, 'How could it explain if it *were* true?' What is it about explanation that guarantees truth? I think there is no plausible answer to this question when one law explains another. But when we reason about theoretical entities the situation is different. The reasoning is causal, and to accept the explanation is to admit the cause. (Cartwright, 1983, p. 99)

---

[26] Recall that it is this feature of mathematics that Putnam so forcefully argued for in his realist days. He argued that mathematical entities feature indispensably in *the very same explanations* that lead realists to believe in theoretical entities. See Putnam (1971) and section 1.2.2.

[27] Elsewhere (1990, p. 7) Ellis is more explicit about his endorsement of a causal theory of knowledge.

In her rejection of inference to the best explanation she aligns herself more with anti-realists such as Bas van Fraassen[28] but accepts theoretical entities that feature in causal explanations for the same sorts of reasons as Ian Hacking.[29] So whereas Ellis is a realist who rejects inference to the best explanation in its most general sense, it's perhaps more appropriate to see Cartwright as an anti-realist who accepts inference to the most likely cause. Hacking's arguments ensure that causal activity is a sufficient condition for ontological commitment, whereas general anti-realist considerations ensure that it is also a necessary condition. Once put this way it is clear, I think, that for me to reply to Cartwright would involve entering into the realist/anti-realist debate, which I said at the outset I was not going to tackle in this work. Nevertheless, I feel obliged to say something in reply to Cartwright, but before I do this I need to clear up an ambiguity in Cartwright's position.

Recall that Cartwright admits theoretical entities that are causes of some phenomena which require explaining. The ambiguity revolves around what constitutes an event (or phenomenon) in need of explanation. For example, suppose that all entities that are causally active are the cause of some event or other. Then Cartwright's inference to the most likely cause may warrant belief in these entities as the most likely causes of their respective events. Notice that nothing here ensures that the entities in question are causally active with us. On the other hand, one could argue that what she takes to be an event in need of explanation must be an event which *we know about*. That seems uncontroversial enough, but now depending on how we spell out the "we know about" claim, it looks as though Cartwright cannot admit causally active entities that are not causally active with us.

As it turns out I think that it is the latter position that Cartwright intends. This can be best seen by considering a case where there is some event, e, which we have no causal contact with and asking the question: What reason does Cartwright have to believe that such an event occurred? One reason would be if we directly observe e or observe a result of e, but this would mean that we have causal contact with e, and this is ruled out by construction. The important question is whether, for Cartwright, there can be any other way of knowing about e. It seems not, given what she says about inference to the best explanation. Recall that inference to the best explanation is not an admissible inference for Cartwright, so it can't be that e explains some other event or phenomena, unless of course e is

---

[28] For details of van Fraassen's rejection of inference to the best explanation, see van Fraassen (1980).

[29] See footnote 2 in this chapter or Hacking (1983) for further details.

the cause of that event or phenomena, and this is also ruled out by con-struction. What other reason can we have to postulate a causally isolated entity on Cartwright's account? I can think of none, so I must conclude that Cartwright is indeed committed to only those entities that are causally active with us.[30] I will now use this reading of Cartwright's position on some examples I have considered previously. These examples will show how Cartwright's position seems unable to give the intuitively correct result in what are fairly uncontroversial cases.

The first example is that of the stars and planets outside of our light cone. These are theoretical entities that are not the cause of anything (that we can observe), so it seems on Cartwright's account they ought not be granted "real" status. As I've mentioned previously, in relation to the epistemically motivated Eleatic Principle (cf. section 3.2), this seems like the wrong answer. Note, however, that I am not claiming that Cartwright is committed to this view, just that to avoid this conclusion will require some additional argument. In the absence of such argument, the undesirable conclusion does seem to follow from inference to the most likely cause alone.

The other example I'd like to reconsider is the case of belief in the existence of germanium prior to 1887. Recall that I assume that there had been no known causal contact with germanium until 1887, but that it was postulated in 1871 on the basis of a "gap" in Mendeleeff's periodic table. It seems Cartwright must deny any good reason to believe in germanium at that time since its causal isolation guarantees that it couldn't have been the cause of anything (that we knew about) and the only appropriate inference she allows is inference to the most likely cause. Again, I trust that your intuitions suggest that this is the wrong answer.

Much more could be said about Cartwright's ontology and, in particular, her inference to the most likely cause, but in the end I find examples such as these give us good reason to suspect that her project cannot be used to support a causal constraint on existence claims.

---

[30] Cartwright has pointed out to me that she could appeal to some other form of inference besides inference to the best explanation to justify belief in causally isolated events and entities. Nothing in her position rules out such a move. Such a move, however, is not open to defenders of the Eleatic Principle interested in restricting the admissible, relevant inferences to inference to the most likely cause. Such a move clearly undermines the Eleatic Principle by (presumably) allowing belief in entities without any restriction on their causal histories.

3.6   The Content of Scientific Theories

Both Jody Azzouni (1997a) and Mark Balaguer (1996b; 1998) have been critical of Quinean naturalism. They have suggested (in different ways) that it is a mistake to read our ontological commitments simply from what the quantifiers of our best scientific theories range over. Rather, we should pay attention to what our best scientific theories are *about* and count only those entities as real. Azzouni and Balaguer argue that our best scientific theories are not about mathematical entities, for instance, but about causally efficacious entities such as electrons, stars, and such. They thus suggest that only the latter causally active entities should be admitted to our ontology.

Although Azzouni's and Balaguer's intuitions are similar—it's the content of the theories that's important, not the domains of quantification—their arguments are different enough to warrant separate consideration. In each case I'll focus attention on the parts of their arguments that might be used to support the Eleatic Principle. I begin with Balaguer.

3.6.1   Balaguer's Fictionalism

Balaguer's position,[31] in a nutshell, is that "the nominalistic content of empirical science is all empirical science is really 'trying to say' about the world" (Balaguer, 1998, p. 141). We thus need not have ontological commitment to anything other than the entities that are part of this nominalistic content—that is, the causally efficacious entities.

Balaguer begins by pointing out that entities that lack causal powers could not make a difference to the way the *physical* world is. He thus defends the view that the content of our scientific theories can be separated into nominalistic and Platonistic components and that the nominalistic content (i.e., the purely physical facts described by such theories) is true (or mostly true), while the Platonistic content (i.e., the abstract, mathematical facts described by such theories) is fictional (1998, p. 131).

To illustrates his position, he considers a scientific claim such as

(A) The physical system S is forty degrees Celsius.

Balaguer argues that while (A) does assert that a certain relation holds

---

[31] I should point out that Balaguer does not ultimately accept the position that I'll be attributing to him in this section. (He adopts a rather anti-metaphysical stance on such questions as the existence of mathematical entities (1998, pp. 151–179).) He has, however, argued rather persuasively for the position I'll be discussing. I think it is fair to say that he has considerable sympathy with the position and he certainly sees it as a position worthy of serious attention.

between S and the number 40, it is reasonable to maintain that since the number 40 is causally inert, the truth of (A) depends on purely nominalistic facts about S and purely Platonistic facts about the natural numbers; Balaguer argues that these two sets of facts hold or don't hold independently of one another. Thus, again it is reasonable to maintain that facts of the one sort obtain, whereas facts of the other sort do not (i.e., the nominalistic content of (A) is true whereas its Platonistic content is fictional). Balaguer claims that we can take this view of the whole of empirical science: empirical science is not true (because there are no abstract objects), but the nominalistic content of empirical science is true (because, as he puts it, "the physical world holds up *its end* of the 'empirical-science bargain'" (1998, p. 134).

Now it is clear that if Balaguer is right about all this, then we have a rather interesting argument for the Eleatic Principle. There are problems, though, with Balaguer's position. For instance, consider Balaguer's argument for the claim that empirical science does not confirm the existence of mathematical objects:

> Empirical science *knows*, so to speak, that mathematical objects are causally inert. That is, it does not assign any causal role to any mathematical entity. Thus, it seems that empirical science *predicts* that the behavior of the physical world is not dependent in any way upon the existence of mathematical objects. But this suggests that what empirical science says about the physical world—that is, its complete picture of the physical world—could be true even if there aren't any mathematical objects. (Balaguer, 1998, p. 133)

It's not at all clear, however, that the physical universe cannot depend upon causally inert (or at least causally isolated) entities. After all, physicists posit causally isolated universes (i.e., universes with no causal influence on *this* universe) in order to explain why our universe is fine-tuned for carbon-based life (Barrow and Tipler, 1986). It seems, then, that certain features of the physical universe (namely, its "fine-tuning") may be explained by appeal to causally isolated entities (i.e., other universes) and thus, in some sense, the physical universe may indeed be said to depend upon causally isolated entities.[32]

In a review of Balaguer (1998), Ed Zalta and I raised a somewhat vague concern about Balaguer's nominalist project (Colyvan and Zalta, 1999). We claimed that Balaguer's driving intuition here—"the nominalistic content of empirical science is all empirical science is really 'trying to say' about

---

[32] In fact, Balaguer seems to be assuming that all explanation is causal. I argued against this position in section 3.3.

the world"—is little more than an intuition in favour of nominalism. We suggested that

> at least part of the business of science is to describe reality. To suppose that reality can be described by the nominalistic content of scientific theories is something akin to begging the question against the Platonist. (Colyvan and Zalta, 1999, p. 344)

Let me now try to flesh out this concern.

It seems to me that there is a very interesting ambiguity in the claim that the nominalistic content is all that science is really trying to say about the world. The ambiguity is appreciated if we consider the following example. Suppose we wish to tell the story of why my hand won't pass through a solid object such as a wall. Now in one sense this story is simply about the wall and my hand. But in another sense, it's (somewhat surprisingly) about quite a bit more, because the explanation of why my hand won't pass through the wall involves a story about the electro-repulsive forces of the electrons in both the wall and my hand. Of course, all we're trying to do is talk about walls and hands, but in doing so we are forced to discuss electrons. The confusion is between what the theory is supposed to be describing or explaining and what resources it requires to do the describing or explaining. Now I think it is clear that there *is* a sense in which the explanation of why my hand will not pass through the wall is simply about hands and walls. This, however, does little to convince us that we have no reason to believe in electrons.[33]

Now the ambiguity that I see in Balaguer's intuition that the nominalistic content is all science is really trying to say is between the following two readings: (1) what science is ultimately trying to describe or explain is simply the nominalistic content and (2) the scientific descriptions and explanations ultimately will not need to appeal to anything other than the nominalistic content. Now Balaguer might well be correct that (1) is true, but it is clear that (2) does not follow from (1). Moreover, my hand, wall, and electron example shows that ontological commitments hang on (2) not (1). If, as I suggest, Balaguer is conflating (1) and (2), his intuition is indeed something akin to begging the question against Platonism. For (2) supposes that our ultimate descriptions and explanations of the world will not require anything other than nominalistic resources. In any case, this is not an intuition that I share.

---

[33] I'm restricting my attention to scientific realists here. Of course, anti-realists such as van Fraassen do reject electrons for reasons along these lines. Balaguer, however, is trying to show that one can be a nominalist and a scientific realist.

3.6.2 Azzouni's Challenge

Let's turn our attention to Azzouni. Although Jody Azzouni has criticised (the letter of) Quinean naturalism in a number of places,[34] I'll focus on Azzouni (1997a) where he comes closest to defending a version of the Eleatic Principle. Azzouni suggests that when we consider a problem such as the movement of two (nearly) homogeneous and (nearly) perfectly spherical masses connected by a spring and tossed up into a gravitational field, we find three quite distinct sorts of objects quantified over. The first are the spheres themselves; the second are items like centres of mass; the third are mathematical quantities (such as the product of the two masses). Now Azzouni suggests that the first category is what the theory is about. The second, although physically significant, is not real and the third category, according to Azzouni, is not even physically significant. He argues that it is only the two spheres that we interact with, not centres of mass and certainly not mathematical entities. The point is that:

> there is in place an implicit causal story about the sorts of objects we interact with. Even when quite sophisticated instruments are involved ... , still, in the physical description of how the instrument does what it does, we find implicit and explicit causal relations described. When such a story is missing, as it invariably is with physically significant items which are not physically real (such as centres of mass) or with merely mathematical objects (such as various functions of physical quantities that we could define), we find no causal interactions with the item (either between it and us, or between it and other physical items). (Azzouni, 1997a, p. 200)

So the suggestion is that scientific theories are about the physically real and these we can causally interact with. Moreover, it is only the physically real that we are ontological committed to.

The problem with this suggestion, however, should be quite familiar by now: There are physically real objects outside our light cone. As we've already seen, we do not causally interact with these, and so they fail the causal test. Azzouni admits that being an item with which we can causally interact is a sufficient but not a necessary condition on being physically real. But this is enough to suggest that Azzouni's proposal is of little use as a defence of an Eleatic Principle. But Azzouni makes a very interesting suggestion. He suggests that causal power might provide a *defeasible* criterion:

---

[34] See, for example, Azzouni (1994; 1997b; 1998; 2000).

Notice that if something is physically real, but out of our causal reach, the physicist will usually have a story for why this is so (e.g., it's too far away). Such a story is unnecessary, and never given, when it comes to centres of mass or purely numerical items. (Azzouni, 1997a, p. 210)

As it turns out, I have a great deal of sympathy with this suggestion. The suggestion is in effect that the Eleatic Principle is not the final arbiter, but a rule of thumb that can be overturned when it gives the wrong results. We know when it gives the wrong results by considering the scientific theory as a whole. Moreover, when the Eleatic Principle gives the wrong result, total theory should provide a story about why we got the wrong result. I will pursue this suggestion further in the next section, where I will argue that this and similar suggestions are very much in the spirit of Quinean naturalism. Of course, there is room for disagreement about when entities with which we have no causal interactions are to be admitted into our ontology and what the story concerning such entities should look like,[35] but for the moment, it is sufficient to simply note that Azzouni's suggestion of a defeasible Eleatic Principle marks a serious departure from the causal version of naturalism under discussion.[36]

3.7   The Moral

In this section I will show that there is a positive message to be gleaned from the lack of support for the Eleatic Principle. In section 3.1 we saw how the inductive argument for the principle is in itself inadequate but leads rather naturally to epistemic considerations. These, in turn, suffer from the same sorts of objections as the causal theory of knowledge (which is, after all, what underlies the epistemic motivation). In particular, we saw how this motivation yields some undesirable consequences in some fairly straight-forward cases; for instance, that we ought not believe in stars and planets

---

[35] For example, Azzouni suggests that there is an important difference between mathematical entities and items outside our light cone. The latter, he suggests, are admitted despite failing the causal test because an explanation for their failure is available. Although mathematical entities also fail, no excuses are offered on their behalf. But it seems that a very good story is available: *Mathematical entities do not have causal powers*. Moreover, that this is so well known explains why in this case "such a story is unnecessary, and never given" (Azzouni, 1997a, p. 210).

[36] I don't want to give the impression that Azzouni sets out and fails to defend the Eleatic Principle. In the article in question (Azzouni, 1997a), at least, he simply explores the cogency of a non-Quinean naturalism (not unlike the causal version we've been considering). Moreover, he does this without providing an argument for the position in question.

outside of our own light cone. Such a position is surely unpalatable to even the staunchest defenders of the principle. In section 3.3 I examined what I take to be the most important argument for the Eleatic Principle, due to David Armstrong. Armstrong claims that causally idle entities have no explanatory value and hence should not be considered to be real. This argument was seen to rely on the assumption that only causally active entities have explanatory power, and this was shown to be a mistake. Finally, in section 3.5 we saw that motivating the Eleatic Principle by appeal to a restriction of inference to the best explanation to causal explanation also faces serious problems.

The moral to be drawn from all this is best illustrated by considering the deficiencies of the arguments for the Eleatic Principle and how they might be overcome. For instance, the epistemic justification failed because it ruled out entities such as germanium prior to 1887 and stars and planets outside our light cone, which seem reasonable to believe in. There is a way of getting around these problem cases though, and that is to appeal to some sort of 'rounding out' principle. Thus, a defender of the causal test may argue that even though an epistemically motivated Eleatic Principle rules out stars and planets outside our light cone, such entities may, nevertheless, be included in our ontology on the basis of this rounding out principle.[37] But now one wonders what the purpose of the Eleatic Principle is, if it is so easily overruled when it gives the wrong answer. Why not try to be more explicit about what the rounding out principle amounts to and just appeal to it in the first place?

It seems this rounding out principle, if it allows belief in stars and planets outside our own light cone, is going to do so for reasons of symmetry or, more generally, for reasons of theoretic virtue. That is, the astronomical theory that posits stars and planets outside our own light cone is a better theory than its counterpart that does not posit such entities. (For one thing, the latter theory is stuck with the problem of explaining why the earth is apparently at the centre of the universe.) Now notice that most entities that are causally active are likely to be needed in (causal) explanations of certain phenomena.[38] Thus, using this rounding out principle, at least as I've outlined it here, will effectively subsume one direction of the Eleatic Principle—causally active entities will gain admission to our ontology because they are needed for our scientific theories. This principle looks more promising than the Eleatic Principle, since it seems to avoid the

---

[37] For instance, in private conversation Alan Musgrave has suggested this. Note also the similarity between this suggestion and Azzouni's suggestion (in section 3.6.2) of a defeasible Eleatic Principle.

[38] For example, the stars and planets inside our own light cone will be needed to explain why we see points of light when we look up at the night sky.

more obvious pitfalls of the epistemically motivated Eleatic Principle and yet, because in many cases both principles yield the same results, it retains much of the Eleatic Principle's intuitive appeal. In effect, I'm suggesting that the Eleatic Principle may be a good ontological "rule of thumb" but may not be the final arbiter on such matters.[39]

Alternatively, let's cast our minds back to the Armstrong argument for the Eleatic Principle. This argument placed the responsibility for questions of ontology firmly upon the explanatory power of the entities in the theories in which they occur. My point of disagreement was that acausal entities also have explanatory power, so we should not confine our attention to causally active entities. I agree that explanations featuring causally active entities are often very good explanations, and perhaps we ought to seek such explanations when appropriate. It's just that it's pointless to restrict our attention to these explanations, since they do not exhaust the acceptable explanations of science. There is, however, an important insight in Armstrong's argument. This insight is the move to using explanatory power as a guide to deciding questions of ontology. If we heed this advice, but do not restrict the acceptable explanations of science to those featuring causally active entities, we find ourselves once again with a very general principle for deciding ontology, not unlike the rounding out principle we arrived at in the last paragraph. In both cases the principle places the responsibility for ontology on theoretic virtue (symmetry in the former case and explanatory power in the latter), and in both cases the principle goes well beyond the scope of the Eleatic Principle.

This more general principle now begins to look very much like Quine's ontic thesis. So, by responding to the difficulties faced by the Eleatic Principle, we are lead to something very much like Quinean naturalism. Now of course this does not mean that Quinean naturalism is the *only* way to avoid these difficulties, but it does at least suggest that the Quinean position is better equipped to embark on the difficult task of deciding which entities we allow entry to our ontology.

---

[39] Indeed, there is some evidence to suggest that even some of the principle's supporters may agree with me here. For instance, in the following passage David Armstrong suggests that the causal criterion is a heuristic device for isolating those entities for which it is hoped that a reductive analysis may be given:

> The argument from lack of causal power is simply intended as a reason for thinking that the research programme [of giving an account of the truth conditions of numbers, classes, propositions etc. in terms of particulars and their properties and relations] is a promising one. (Armstrong, 1978, Vol. 2, p. 5)

In other words, he suspects that causally idle entities are dispensable to science but admits that the real work is the required reduction of such entities to more respectable entities.

3.8 Recapitulation

So far I have discussed the Quine/Putnam indispensability argument and shown how it depends on the Quinean doctrines of naturalism and holism. I then defended the Quinean reading of naturalism against causal versions of naturalism. The latter explicitly or implicitly appeal to a causal test in order to decide which entities are legitimately deserving of real status, with only the causally active entities able to pass this test. In this chapter I argued against the use of such a test.

It is important to see the problems associated with such a test for at least two reasons. First, assuming that it is desirable to hold some version of naturalism, discrediting the causal version raises the stocks in its main rival: Quinean naturalism. The second reason is that in considering the problems with the Eleatic Principle and how they might be rectified, we found that one is drawn in a very natural way to Quinean indispensability theory. None of this counts as a positive argument for the Quinean position; indeed, as is often the case with such basic doctrinal beliefs, it is difficult to produce persuasive positive arguments. The best one can hope for is that the doctrine in question fare well in cost–benefit comparisons with the main contenders. I hope you agree that the preceding chapters have shown that the Quinean position, if not the best approach to matters of ontology, is at least highly plausible.

Much more could be said concerning the Quinean backdrop, particularly with regard to naturalism, but instead I shall move on to consider some explicit attacks on the indispensability argument. In discussing these attacks, however, issues concerning the Quinean backdrop will arise again. This will hopefully bring into sharper focus the doctrines of naturalism and holism and underline their importance to the whole debate.

4

Field's Fictionalism

The indispensability argument has suffered attacks from seemingly all directions in recent times. First Charles Chihara (1973) and Hartry Field (1980) raised doubts about the indispensability of mathematics to science, then more recently Elliot Sober (1993) and Penelope Maddy (1992; 1995; 1998b) have expressed concerns as to whether we really ought to be committed to entities that are indispensable to our best scientific theories. In the next three chapters I will address some of these objections, and I'll show that the indispensability argument can survive these attacks.

I begin in this chapter by considering the influential work of Hartry Field. Although there are other nominalist philosophies of mathematics addressing the indispensability argument,[1] I shall restrict my attention to Field's distinctive fictionalism. There are many reasons for this, not least of which is the considerable influence Field's work has had on the literature in the 20 years since the publication of *Science Without Numbers* (Field, 1980). This influence is no accident; it's a tribute to the plausibility of the account of mathematics offered by Field and his unwillingness to dodge the issues associated with the applications of mathematics. Furthermore, unlike other nominalist philosophies of mathematics,[2] Field's nominalism is not revisionist:

> I do not propose to reinterpret any part of classical mathematics; instead, I propose to show that the mathematics needed for

---

[1] See Burgess and Rosen (1997) for detailed discussion of the various nominalist programs.

[2] For example, see Chihara (1973), where mathematical discourse is *reinterpreted* so as to be about linguistic entities rather than mathematical entities.

> application to the physical world does not include anything which
> even *prima facie* contains references to (or quantifications over) ab-
> stract entities like numbers, functions, or sets. Towards that part
> of mathematics which does contain references to (or quantification
> over) abstract entities—and this includes virtually all of conventional
> mathematics—I adopt a fictional attitude: that is, I see no reason to
> regard this part of mathematics as *true*. (Field, 1980, pp. 1–2)

He accepts the Quinean backdrop discussed in chapter 2 and agrees that
if mathematics were indispensable to our best scientific theories, we would
have good cause to grant mathematical entities real status, but he denies
that mathematics is indispensable to science. In effect he accepts the burden of proof in this debate. That is, he accepts that he must show (1) how
it is that mathematical discourse may be used in its various applications in
physical science and (2) that it is possible to do science without reference
to mathematical entities. This is indeed an ambitious project and certainly
one deserving careful attention, for if it succeeds, indispensability theory is
no longer a way of motivating mathematical realism.

Given that I am committed to a defence of the indispensability argument, it may come as some surprise to find that my disagreements with
Field are rather slight. We both accept the Quinean backdrop of holism
and naturalism; we both agree that the indispensability argument is a good
argument—indeed, we both agree that it is the only good argument for Platonism; we both agree that if mathematics can be shown to be dispensable
to science (and its utility to science adequately explained), then we would
have no reason to believe in the existence of mathematical entities. What
we disagree on is the question of whether mathematics is or is not dispensable to science. We both believe that this last issue is still open, but whereas
Field thinks enough of the nominalisation of science has been carried out
to warrant the tentative conclusion that mathematics is dispensable, I'm
inclined to think more work needs to be done to warrant such a conclusion
(even tentatively). In this chapter I hope to make clear what some of this
further work is.

4.1   The Science without Numbers Project

Before discussing the details of Field's project, it is important to understand
something of its motivation. Field is driven by two things. First, there are
well known prima facie difficulties with Platonism—namely, the two Benacerraf problems mentioned in the first chapter (which will be discussed in
more detail in the final chapter)—which nominalism avoids (Field, 1989,

p. 6).[3] Second, he is motivated by certain rather attractive principles in the philosophy of science: (1) we ought to seek *intrinsic* explanations whenever this is possible and (2) we ought to eliminate arbitrariness from theories (Field, 1980, p. ix). In relation to (1), Field says, "one wants to be able to explain the behaviour of the physical system *in terms of the intrinsic features of that system*, without invoking extrinsic entities (whether non-mathematical or mathematical) whose properties are irrelevant to the behaviour of the system being explained" (emphasis in original) (Field, 1984, p. 193). He also points out that this concern is orthogonal to nominalism (Field, 1980, p. 44). As for (2), this too is independent of nominalism. Coordinate-independent (tensor) methods used in most field theories are considered more attractive by Platonists and nominalists alike. The importance of these motivations will arise in the course of this chapter. At this stage it is sufficient to note them and, in particular, to realise that his project is driven by more than just nominalist concerns.

Now to the details of Field's project. There are two parts to the project. The first is to justify the use of mathematics in its various applications in empirical science. If one is to present a believable, fictional account of mathematics, one must present some account of how mathematics may be used with such effectiveness in its various applications in physical theories. To do this, Field argues that mathematical theories don't have to be true to be useful in applications; they merely need to be *conservative*. This is, roughly, that if a mathematical theory is added to a nominalist scientific theory, no nominalist consequences follow that wouldn't follow from the scientific theory alone. I'll have more to say about this shortly. The second part of his program is to demonstrate that our best scientific theories can be suitably nominalised. To do this, he is content to nominalise a large fragment of Newtonian gravitational theory. Although this is a far cry from showing that *all* our *current* best scientific theories can be nominalised, it is certainly not trivial. The hope is that once one sees how the elimination of reference to mathematical entities can be achieved for a typical physical theory, it will seem plausible that the project could be completed for the rest of science.

One further point that is important to bear in mind is that Field is interested in undermining what he takes to be the only good argument for Platonism. He is thus justified in using Platonistic methods. His strategy is to show *Platonistically* that abstract entities are not needed in order to do empirical science. If his program is successful, "[P]latonism is left in an unstable position: it entails its own unjustifiability" (Field, 1980, p. 6). I'll

---

[3] Or, rather, nominalism trades these problems for a different set of problems—most notably, to disarm the indispensability argument.

now discuss the first part of his program.

4.1.1   Conservativeness

Field's account of how it is that mathematical theories might be used in scientific theories, even when the mathematical theory in question is false, is crucial to his fictional account of mathematics. Field, of course, does provide such an account, the key to which is the concept of *conservativeness*, which may be defined (roughly) as follows:

Definition 1 (Conservativeness) *A mathematical theory M is said to be conservative if, for any body of nominalistic assertions S and any particular nominalistic assertion C, then C is not a consequence of M + S unless it is a consequence of S.*

A few comments are warranted here in relation to definition 1. First, as it stands, the definition is not quite right; it needs refinement in order to avoid certain technical difficulties. For example, we need to exclude the possibility of the nominalistic theory containing the assertion that there are no abstract entities. Such a situation would render $M + S$ inconsistent. There are natural ways of performing the refinements required, but the details aren't important here. (See Field (1980, pp. 11–12) for details.)[4] Second, "nominalistic assertion" is taken to mean an assertion in which all the variables are explicitly restricted to non-mathematical entities (for reasons I suggested earlier). Third, Field is at times a little unclear about whether he is speaking of semantic entailment or syntactic entailment (e.g., Field (1980, pp. 16–19)); in other places (e.g., Field (1980, p. 40, footnote 30) and Field (1985)) he is explicit that it *is* semantic entailment he is concerned with.[5] Finally, the key concept of conservativeness is closely related to (semantic) consistency.[6] Field, however, cannot (and does not) cash out consistency in model-theoretic terms (as is usually the case), for obviously such a construal depends on models, and these are not available to a nominalist. Instead, Field appeals to a primitive sense of possibility.[7]

Now if it could be proved that all of mathematics were conservative, then its truth or falsity would be irrelevant to its use in empirical science.

---

[4] There are, however, more serious worries about Field's formulation of the conservativeness claim. See Urquhart (1990) for details.

[5] Of course, this is irrelevant if the logic in question is first-order. But since Field was at one stage committed to second-order logic, the semantic versus syntactic entailment issue is important. See Shapiro (1983) and Field (1985) for further details. See also footnote 13 of this chapter.

[6] Conservativeness entails consistency and, in fact, conservativeness can be defined in terms of consistency.

[7] This last point will be important for the discussion of section 6.4.

More specifically, if some mathematical theory were false but conservative, it would not lead to false nominalistic assertions when conjoined with some •nominalist, empirical theory, unless such false assertions were consequences of the empirical theory alone. As Field puts it, "mathematics does not need to be true to be good" (1985, p. 125). Put figuratively, conservativeness ensures that the alleged falsity of the mathematical theory does not "infect" the whole theory.

Field provides a number of reasons for thinking that mathematical theories are conservative. These reasons include several formal proofs of the conservativeness of set theory.[8] Here I just wish to demonstrate the plausibility of the conservativeness claim by showing how closely related conservativeness is to consistency. First, for pure set theory (i.e., set theory without urelements[9]) conservativeness follows from consistency alone (Field, 1980, p. 13). In the case of impure set theory, the conservativeness claim is a little stronger than consistency. An impure set theory could be consistent but fail to be conservative because it implied conclusions about concrete entities that were not logically true. Field sums up the situation (emphasis in original):

> [S]tandard mathematics *might* turn out not to be conservative ... , for it might conceivably turn out to be inconsistent, and if it is inconsistent it certainly isn't conservative. We would however regard a proof that standard mathematics was inconsistent as extremely surprising, and as showing that standard mathematics needed revision. Equally, it would be extremely surprising if it were to be discovered that standard mathematics implied that there are at least 10^6 non-mathematical objects in the universe, or that the Paris Commune was defeated; and were such a discovery to be made, all but the most unregenerate rationalists would take this as showing that standard mathematics needed revision. *Good* mathematics *is* conservative; a discovery that accepted mathematics isn't conservative would be a discovery that it isn't good. (Field, 1980, p. 13)

It is also worth noting that Field claims that there is a disanalogy here between mathematical theories and theories about unobservable physical entities. The latter he suggests *do* facilitate new conclusions about observables and hence are not conservative (Field, 1980, p. 10). This disanalogy is due to the fact that conservativeness is also closely related to necessary truth. In fact, conservativeness follows from necessary truth. Field's remark that "[c]onservativeness might loosely be thought of as 'necessary

---

[8] See Field (1980, pp. 16–19) and Field (1992) for details.

[9] A urelement is an element of a set that is not itself a set.

truth without the truth'" (Field, 1988, p. 241) is very helpful. As is the following diagram (which I borrow from Field (1988, p. 241)), illustrating the relevant relationships:

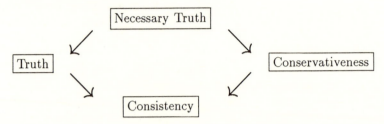

With conservativeness established then, it is permissible for a fictionalist about mathematics to use mathematics in a nominalistic theory, despite the falsity of the former. It remains to show that our current best scientific theories can be purged of their references to abstract objects. I'll discuss Field's treatment of this in the next section.

4.1.2 Nominalisation

Field's strategy for eliminating all references to mathematical objects from empirical science is to appeal to the representation theorems of measurement theory. Although the details of this are fairly technical, no account of Field's program is complete without at least an indication of how this is done. It is also of considerable interest in its own right. Furthermore, as Michael Resnik points out, this part of his program provides a very nice account of applied mathematics, which should be of interest to *all* philosophers of mathematics, realists and anti-realists alike (Resnik, 1983, p. 515). In light of all this, it would be remiss of me not to at least outline this part of Field's program, despite its limited significance to the main thrust of this book. (Those readers not interested in the technical details, can skip ahead to section 4.2 without any loss of continuity.)

Perhaps the most accessible example of a representation theorem is seen in Hilbert's axiomatisation of Euclidean geometry (Hilbert (1899)), on which Field's program is modelled. The central idea is to replace all talk of distance and location, which require quantification over real numbers, with the comparative predicates "between" and "congruent," which require only quantification over space-time points. It will be instructive to present this case in a little more detail. My treatment here follows Field (1980, pp. 24–29).

For my purposes, the important feature of Hilbert's theory is that it contains the following relations:

1. The three-place *between* relation (where 'y' is between 'x' and 'z' is written '$y\,\mathrm{Bet}\,xz$'), which is intuitively understood to mean that x is a point on the line segment with endpoints y and z.

2. The four-place *segment-congruence* relation (where 'x and y are congruent to z and w' is written '$xy\,\mathrm{Cong}\,zw$'), which is intuitively understood to mean that the distance from point x to point y is the same as the distance from point z to point w.

The notion of (Euclidean) distance appealed to in the segment-congruence relation is *not* part of Hilbert's theory; in fact, it cannot even be defined in the theory. But this does not mean that Hilbert's theory is deficient in any sense, for he proved in a broader mathematical theory the following representation theorem:

Theorem 1 (Hilbert's Representation Theorem) *For any model of Hilbert's axiom system for space S, there exists a function* $\mathrm{d} : S \times S \rightarrow \mathbb{R}^+ \cup \{0\}$ *which satisfies the following two homomorphism conditions:*

(a) For any four points x, y, z, and w, $xy\,\mathrm{Cong}\,zw$ iff $\mathrm{d}(xy) = \mathrm{d}(zw)$;

(b) For any three points x, y, and z, $y\,\mathrm{Bet}\,xz$ iff $\mathrm{d}(xy) + \mathrm{d}(yz) = \mathrm{d}(xz)$.

From this it is easy to show that any Euclidean theorem about length would be true if restated as a theorem about any function d satisfying the conditions of theorem 1. In this way we can replace quantification over numbers with quantification over points. As Field puts it (emphasis in original):

> So *in the geometry itself* we can't talk about numbers, and hence we can't talk about distances ... ; but we have a metatheoretic proof which associates claims about distances ... with what we can say in the theory. Numerical claims then, are abstract counterparts of purely geometric claims, and the equivalence of the abstract counterpart with what it is an abstract counterpart of is established in the broader mathematical theory. (Field, 1980, p. 27)

Hilbert also proved a uniqueness theorem corresponding to theorem 1. This theorem states that if there are two functions d_1 and d_2 satisfying the conditions of theorem 1, then $\mathrm{d}_1 = k\mathrm{d}_2$ where k is some arbitrary positive constant. This, claims Field, provides a satisfying explanation of why geometric laws formulated in terms of distance are invariant under multiplication by a positive constant (and that this is the only transformation under which they are invariant). Field claims that this is one of the advantages of this approach: The invariance is given an explanation in terms of the intrinsic facts about space (Field, 1980, p.27). I'll have more to say about this later in the chapter.

With the example of Hilbert's axiomatisation of Euclidean space in hand, Field then does for Newtonian space-time what Hilbert did for $\mathbb{R}^2$. This in itself is non-trivial, but Field is required to do much more, since he must dispense with *all* mention of physical quantities. He does this by appeal to relational properties, which compare space-time points with respect to the quantity in question. For example, rather than saying that some space-time point has a certain gravitational potential, Field compares space-time points with respect to the "greater gravitational potential" relation.[10] The details of this and the more technical task of how to formulate differential equations involving scalar quantities (such as gravitational potential) in terms of the spatial and scalar relational primitives need not concern us here. (The details can be found in Field (1980, pp. 55–91).) The important point is that Field is able to derive an extended representation theorem that, for the sake of completeness, I state here without further comment:[11]

Theorem 2 (Field's Extended Representation Theorem) *For any model of a theory N with space-time S that uses comparative predicates but not numerical functors there are:*

(a) *a 1–1 spatio-temporal co-ordinate function* $\Phi : S \to \mathbb{R}^4$, *which is unique up to generalised Galilean transformation,*

(b) *a mass density function* $\rho : S \to \mathbb{R}^+ \cup \{0\}$, *which is unique up to a positive multiplicative transformation, and*

(c) *a gravitation potential function* $\Psi : S \to \mathbb{R}$, *which is unique up to positive linear transformation,*

all of which are structure preserving (in the sense that the comparative relations defined in terms of these functions coincide with the comparative relations used in N); moreover, the laws of Newtonian gravitational theory in their functorial form hold if Φ, ρ, *and* Ψ *are taken as denotations of the relevant functors.*

We have now seen enough to get the flavour of Field's program, so I'll move on to discuss some related philosophical issues.

---

[10] Of course there is the task of getting the axiomatisation of the gravitational potential relation such that the desired representation and uniqueness theorems are forthcoming. But much of Field's work has, in effect, been done for him by workers in measurement theory (Field, 1980, pp. 57–58).

[11] The statement of the theorem here is from Field (1985, pp. 130–131).

There are many complaints against Field's program, ranging from the complaint that it is not genuinely nominalist (Resnik (1985a; 1985b)) since it makes use of space-time points, to technical difficulties such as the complaint that it is hard to see how Field's program can be made to work for general relativity where the space-time manifold has non-constant curvature (Urquhart, 1990, p. 151) and for theories where the represented objects are not space-time points, but mathematical objects (Malament (1982)).[12] Other complaints revolve around issues concerning the appropriate logic for the project—should it be first- or second-order?—and various problems associated with each option.[13] While such debates are of considerable interest, I will not discuss them further here; they have been dealt with adequately elsewhere by others and I have nothing new to contribute to the debates in question.[14] Instead, I wish to take up the issue of exactly what is required of Field's program. This issue is occasionally confused in the literature, where it is sometimes claimed that Field's program is simply that of *eliminating* quantification over mathematical entities.[15] Although Field does appreciate that the goal of the program is more than that of *elimination*, the point is important and worth stressing for the benefit of some of his supporters.

The problem is that it is not clear how the word "indispensable" is to be understood in this debate. In order to understand just what is required of a program like Field's, then, or indeed to understand the full force of the indispensability argument, we must first clear up what we mean by "indispensable." I shall discuss this in some detail in the following section.

---

[12] For example, in classical Hamiltonian mechanics the represented objects are possible dynamical states. Similar problems, it seems, will arise in any "phase-space" theory, and the prospects look even dimmer for quantum mechanics (Malament, 1982, pp. 533–534). See also Balaguer (1996a) for an indication of how the nominalisation of quantum mechanics might proceed.

[13] See, for example, Shapiro (1983), Urquhart (1990), and Maddy (1990b; 1990c) in this regard. See also Field (1990), where Field seemingly retreats from his earlier endorsement of second-order logic as a result of subsequent debate. The interested reader is also referred to Burgess and Rosen (1997, especially pp. 118–123 and pp. 190–196) for a nice survey and discussion of criticisms of Field's project. I'd like to thank an anonymous reader for Oxford University Press for bringing some of this material to my attention.

[14] It is probably fair to say that the consensus of informed opinion on Field's program is that the various technical difficulties it faces leave a serious question over its likely success. See footnote 13 for relevant references.

[15] For instance, David Papineau (1993) seems to endorse this view when he suggests that the nominalisation part of Field's program requires describing the natural world without mentioning abstract objects (p. 193).

4.2   What Is It to Be Indispensable?

Recall that the indispensability argument may be stated as follows: We have good reason to believe our best scientific theories and there are no grounds on which to differentiate scientific entities from mathematical entities, so we have good reason to believe in mathematical entities, since they, like the relevant scientific entities, are indispensable to the theories in which they occur. Furthermore, it is exactly the same evidence that confirms the scientific theory as a whole, that confirms the mathematical portion of the theory and hence the mathematical entities contained therein. We have just seen that part of Field's program is to show that mathematics is in fact dispensable to science. He begins this task by giving a nominalistic treatment of Newtonian gravitational theory, thus allegedly showing that mathematical entities are dispensable to this theory. This is the point that motivates the present section. He does not give a clear account of what he takes "dispensable" to mean in this context. He clearly does not take it to mean simply eliminable,[16] and yet most of his work is devoted to showing that mathematical entities are eliminable from physical theories.

This failure to explicate what is meant by "indispensable" in Quine's argument allows programs such as Field's to look more attractive than they perhaps ought.[17] In order to come to a clear understanding of how "indispensability" is to be understood, I will consider a case where there should be no disagreement about the dispensability of the entity in question. I shall then analyse this case to see what leads us to conclude that the entity in question is dispensable.

Consider an empirically adequate and consistent theory Γ and let "ξ" be the name of some entity neither mentioned, predicted, or ruled out by Γ. Clearly we can construct a new theory Γ^+ from Γ by simply adding the sentence "ξ exists" to Γ. It is reasonable to suppose that ξ plays no role in the theory Γ^+;[18] it is merely predicted by it. I propose that there should be no disagreement here when I say that ξ is dispensable to Γ^+, but let us

---

[16] For example, in *Science Without Numbers* Field suggests that mathematical entities are theoretically dispensable since "we can give *attractive* reformulations of [the theories of modern physics] in which mathematical entities play no role" (my emphasis) (Field, 1980, p. 8).

[17] Quine actually speaks of entities existentially quantified over in the canonical form of our best theories, rather than indispensability. (See Quine (1948) for details.) Still, the debate continues in terms of *indispensability*, so we would be well served to clarify this latter term.

[18] The reason I hedge a bit here is that if Γ asserts that all entities have positive mass, for instance, then the existence of ξ helps account for some of the "missing mass" of the universe. Thus, ξ *does* play a role in Γ^+. I know of no way of ruling out such cases; hence the hedge.

investigate why this is so.

On one interpretation of "dispensable" we could argue that ξ is not dispensable since its removal from Γ^+ results in a different theory, namely, Γ. This is not a very helpful interpretation though, since *all* entities are indispensable to the theories in which they occur under this reading. Another interpretation of "dispensable" might be that ξ is dispensable to Γ^+ since there exists another theory, Γ, with the same empirical adequacy as Γ^+ in which ξ does not occur.[19] This interpretation can also be seen to be inadequate since it may turn out that *no* theoretical entities are indispensable under this reading. This result follows from Craig's theorem.[20] If the vocabulary of the theory can be partitioned in the way that Craig's theorem requires (cf. footnote 20), then the theory can be reaxiomatised so that any given theoretical entity is eliminated.[21] I claim, therefore, that this interpretation of "dispensable" is unacceptable since it fails to account for why ξ in particular is dispensable.

This leads to the following explication of "dispensable":

Definition 2 (Dispensable) *An entity is dispensable to a theory iff the following two conditions hold:*

(1) There exists a modification of the theory in question resulting in a second theory with exactly the same observational consequences as the first, in which the entity in question is neither mentioned nor predicted.

(2) The second theory must be preferable to the first.

In the preceding example, then, ξ is dispensable since Γ makes no mention of ξ and Γ is preferable to Γ^+ in that the former has less ontological commitment than the latter, all other things being equal. (Assuming, of course, that less ontological commitment is better.[22])

---

[19] Modulo my concerns in footnote 18.

[20] This theorem states that relative to a partition of the vocabulary of an axiomatisable theory T into two classes, τ and ω (theoretical and observational say), there exists an axiomatisable theory T' in the language whose only non-logical vocabulary is ω, of all and only the consequences of T that are expressible in ω alone.

[21] Naturally the question of whether such partitioning is possible is important and somewhat controversial. Quine (arguably) would deny that such a partition is possible. If he is right about this, it will be considerably more difficult to eliminate theoretical entities from scientific theories. I'm willing to grant for the sake of argument, at least, that such a partitioning *is* possible.

[22] One way in which you might think that less ontological commitment is *not* better, is if ξ actually exists. In this case it seems that Γ^+ is the better theory since it best describes reality. This, however, is to gloss over the important question of how we come to know that ξ exists. If there is some evidence of ξ's existence, then Γ^+ will indeed be

Now, it might be argued that on this reading once again every theoretical entity is dispensable, since by Craig's theorem we can eliminate
any reference to any entity and the resulting theory will be better, since
it doesn't have ontological commitment to the entity in question. This argument is flawed though, since the reason for preferring one theory over
another is a complicated question—it is not simply a matter of empirical
adequacy combined with a principle of ontological parsimony. In the next
section I will discuss some aspects of confirmation theory and what role it
plays in indispensability decisions.

4.3   The Role of Confirmation Theory

We can think of confirmation theory as the study of those principles that
guide scientific reasoning other than reasoning of the deductive kind. In
particular, it will help us in deciding whether one theory is better than
another by giving us some desiderata for "good theories."

First and foremost, a good theory must be empirically adequate; that
is, it must agree with all (or at least most) observation. Second, it must
be consistent, both internally and with other major theories. This is not
the whole story though. As we have already seen, Γ and Γ^+ have the same
degree of empirical adequacy and consistency (by construction), and yet we
are inclined to prefer the former over the latter. I am in agreement with
many authors here[23] that among the additional features we require are the
following:

(1) **Simplicity/Parsimony:** Given two theories with the same empirical adequacy, we generally prefer that theory which is simpler both
in its statement and in its ontological commitments. For example,
Einstein, in his formulation of the special theory of relativity, refused
to admit an undetectable luminiferous ether, as some rival theories
did, to jointly explain the propagation of electromagnetic radiation
through apparently empty space and the failure of the Michelson-
Morley experiment to detect such an ether (Einstein, 1905, p. 38).

---

the better theory, since it will be empirically superior. If there is no such evidence for
the existence of ξ, then it seems entirely reasonable to prefer Γ over Γ^+ as I suggest. It
is the latter I had in mind when I set up this case. Indeed, the former case is ruled out
by construction. I am not concerned with whether ξ actually exists or not—just that
there be no empirical evidence for it.

[23] See, for instance, Hempel (1965, pp. 203–206), Horwich (1982, pp. 1–15), Weinberg
(1993, pp. 105–131), Glymour (1980, pp. 152–155), and Quine (1960a). While all these
authors wouldn't agree with my characterisation of the additional features entirely, I
think I have captured what are the most common elements in all their accounts.

(2) **Unificatory/Explanatory Power:** Philip Kitcher (1981) argues rather convincingly for scientific explanation being unification; that is, accounting for a maximum of observed phenomena with a minimum of theoretical devices. Whether or not you accept Kitcher's account, we still require that a theory not simply predict certain phenomena, but explain why such predictions are expected. Furthermore, the best theories do so with a minimum of theoretical devices. For example, the success of Newtonian gravitational theory was in no small way due to its ability to explain such diverse phenomena as tides, planetary orbits, and projectile motion (among other things) from a small stock of theoretical "machinery."

(3) **Boldness/Fruitfulness:** We expect our best theories not to simply predict everyday phenomena, but to make bold predictions of novel entities and phenomena that lead to fruitful future research. The prediction of gravitational waves by general relativity is an example of a bold prediction that is still being actively investigated.

(4) **Formal Elegance:** This is perhaps the hardest feature to characterise (and no doubt the most contentious). However, there is at least *some* sense in which our best theories have aesthetic appeal. For instance, it may well be on the grounds of formal elegance that we rule out ad hoc modifications to a failing theory.

I will not argue in detail for each of these, except to say that despite the notorious difficulties involved in explicating what we mean by such terms as "simplicity" and "elegance," most scientific realists at least do look for such virtues in our best theories.[24] Otherwise, we could never choose between two theories such as Γ and Γ^+. I do not claim that this list is comprehensive nor do I claim that it is minimal;[25] I merely claim that these sorts of criteria are typically appealed to in the literature to distinguish good theories and I have no objection to such appeals.

In the light of the preceding discussion then, we see that to claim that an entity is dispensable is to claim that a modification of the theory in which it is posited can be made in such a way as to eliminate the entity in question and result in a theory that is better overall (or at least not worse) in terms of simplicity, elegance, and so on. Thus, we see that the argument I presented at the end of the previous section that *any* theoretical entity is dispensable does indeed fail, as I claimed. This is because in most cases the

[24] And the main target of the indispensability argument is scientific realists.

[25] For instance, it may be possible to explain formal elegance in terms of simplicity and unificatory power.

benefit of ontological simplicity obtained by the elimination of the entity in question will be more than offset by losses in other areas.

While it seems reasonable to suppose that the elimination from the body of scientific theory of physical entities such as electrons would cause an overall reduction in the previously described virtues of that theory, it is not so clear that the elimination of mathematical entities would have the same impact. Someone might argue that mathematics is certainly a very effective language for the expression of scientific ideas, in that it simplifies the calculations and statement of much of science, but to do so at the expense of introducing into one's ontology the whole gamut of mathematical entities simply isn't a good deal.

One response to this is to deny that it is a high price at all. After all, a powerful and efficient language is the cornerstone of any good theory. If you have to introduce a few more entities into the theory to get it, then so be it. Although I have considerable sympathy with this response, here I wish to pursue a different and, I think, a more convincing line. I will argue that mathematics plays an *active* role in many of the theories that make use of it. That is, it is not just a tool that makes calculations easier or simplifies the statement of the theory; it makes important contributions to all of the desiderata of good theories I mentioned earlier.[26]

My strategy from here is to show that there is good reason to believe that the mathematised version of a theory is more "virtuous" than the unmathematised theory, and so there is good reason to believe mathematics is indispensable to our best physical theories. I shall demonstrate this in the next section by appealing to a number of examples of physical theories and showing how the mathematised theory is capable of more than what one would expect from a nominalised version. Notice that it is not necessary for me to show that this is the case for *all* our best physical theories, as the indispensability argument goes through in case mathematics is indispensable to some non-empty subset of our best physical theories.

I also note here that I am not proposing to *prove* the indispensability of mathematics in the cases I consider, merely to suggest that if these theories were stripped of their mathematical content it seems that they would lose much of their appeal. If I succeed, then the burden of proof lies with anyone who claims that mathematics *is* dispensable, for they must show, first, how it is possible to remove all commitment to mathematical entities from all physical theories, and second, how this removal does not result in a

---

[26] The mathematical physicist Freeman Dyson (1964) makes a similar point when he says "mathematics is not just a tool by means of which phenomena can be calculated; it is the main source of concepts and principles by means of which new theories can be created" (p. 129).

reduction of the virtue of these theories. This problem will be particularly evident in the cases I consider in the next section.

4.4 The Role of Mathematics in Physical Theories

David Papineau claims that "the incorporation of pure mathematics into scientific theories ... might make it easier to do calculations, but ... receives no backing from principles of scientific theory choice" (1993, p. 196). In this section I will show that this view is, at the very least, extremely controversial. I will demonstrate this by appealing to a number of examples in which mathematics contributes to the unification and boldness of the physical theory in question, and therefore *is* supported by well-recognised principles of scientific theory choice.[27]

4.4.1 The Complex Numbers

The first example is the complex numbers. I will show how the introduction of these was responsible for a great deal of unification within both pure mathematics and in more practical areas such as differential equations in physics.

Perhaps the most profound use of complex numbers is in the theory of integration of complex valued functions of a complex variable; in particular, in providing a method for the exact evaluation of many real integrals that are unobtainable by other methods.[28] This, however, would take us too far into the theory of complex analysis for our purposes. Instead, I wish to look at a simpler application of complex numbers: the unification of the exponential and trigonometric functions. This has direct applications in the study of second-order ordinary differential equations. These arise in almost all branches of science, including fluid mechanics, heat conduction, and population dynamics.

We begin by introducing the number $i = \sqrt{-1}$ and defining a complex variable $z = x + yi$ where x and y are real. Once we have extended the operations '$+$' and '$\cdot$' and the relation '$=$' from the reals to the complex in the natural way, we can introduce complex exponentiation via the following

---

[27] We might also ask Papineau why social scientists and others are so hell-bent on mathematising their theories if so doing has no impact on theory choice.

[28] I am referring here to the remarkable Cauchy integral formula and the like. See Ahlfors's (1966) classic treatment of this subject.

equation, known as Euler's formula:

$$e^{i\theta} = \cos\theta + i\sin\theta \quad \theta \in \mathbb{R}.$$

From this we can define the trigonometric functions for a complex variable z as

$$\sin z = \frac{e^{iz} - e^{-iz}}{2i} \quad \text{and} \quad \cos z = \frac{e^{iz} + e^{-iz}}{2}.$$

The usual real-valued sine and cosine functions are then seen to be special cases. Thus, the complex numbers are instrumental in the unification of the trigonometric and the exponential functions. This unification, being within mathematics itself, may seem somewhat artificial, so I shall demonstrate how this unification "flows through" to physics.

Consider the second-order linear homogeneous ordinary differential equation with constant coefficients:

$$y'' + y' + y = 0 \tag{4.1}$$

where y is a real-valued function of the single real variable x. Equations such as these are ubiquitous in physics—they describe many physical systems such as the flow of fluids through pipes, electromagnetism, and population growth. They are solved by considering their respective characteristic equations, which are quadratics and so, by the fundamental theorem of algebra, always have two (complex) roots (counting multiplicity). In this case the characteristic equation is

$$r^2 + r + 1 = 0$$

which has roots $r = -\frac{1}{2} \pm i\frac{\sqrt{3}}{2}$. Now the general solution to an equation with unequal roots to its characteristic equation is

$$y = c_1 e^{r_1 x} + c_2 e^{r_2 x} \tag{4.2}$$

where c_1 and c_2 are arbitrary real constants and r_1 and r_2 are the two distinct roots of the characteristic equation.[29] Note that (4.2) is indifferent as to whether r_1 and r_2 are real or complex. Thus, the solution to (4.1) is given by

$$y = c_1 e^{(-\frac{1}{2} + \frac{\sqrt{3}}{2}i)x} + c_2 e^{(-\frac{1}{2} - \frac{\sqrt{3}}{2}i)x}$$

---

[29] See Boyce and DiPrima (1986) for further details.

which reduces to the *real* solution

$$y = e^{\frac{-x}{2}} \left(c_1 \cos \left(\frac{\sqrt{3}}{2} x \right) + c_2 \sin \left(\frac{\sqrt{3}}{2} x \right) \right)$$

due to Euler's formula given previously.

So we see that without the use of complex numbers we would have to treat the equations $y'' - y = 0$, which has real roots to its characteristic equation, quite differently from $y'' + y = 0$, which has complex roots to its characteristic equation. Furthermore, the connection between the exponential function, which is a solution to the first, and the cosine and sine functions, which are solutions to the second, is spelled out via the definitions of trigonometric functions of a complex variable given earlier. This I see as a fine example of the unity a mathematical theory may bring not only to other mathematical theories but also to scientific theory as a whole.

What is more, I take this unity to be not simply an algorithmic unity; that is, a single method for finding solutions to these equations. Rather, I take it that the algorithmic unity arises out of deep structural similarities between the systems portrayed by these equations. For example, if two different physical systems are governed by the same differential equation, it's clear that there is some similarity between these systems, no matter how disparate the systems may seem (just as a red planet and a red pepper have something in common). It seems plausible, at least, that this similarity is structural and is captured by the relevant differential equation. Even when the systems are governed by different differential equations, structural similarities may still be revealed in the mathematics. In the case of the two equations in the previous paragraph, the structural similarity of any two systems governed by these equations is revealed by the connection between the equations' respective solutions. Mathematics, because of its abstract nature, is extremely well suited to providing unification in this very important sense.

4.4.2 The Dirac Equation

The next example is a case where the mathematical component of the theory played an active part in the prediction of novel phenomena—in this case the discovery of antimatter. Here, however, there was reason to doubt the predictions because the solutions to the equations involved didn't seem to have any physical representation.[30]

---

[30] Mark Steiner (1989) discusses this example in a slightly different context. See Steiner (1989; 1998) for other interesting examples of the important role mathematics plays in physical theory. See also Baker (forthcoming).

In classical physics one occasionally comes across solutions to equations that are discarded because they are taken to be "non-physical." Examples include negative energy solutions to dynamical systems. This situation arose for Paul Dirac in 1928 when he was studying the solutions of the equation of relativistic quantum mechanics that now bears his name. This equation describes the behaviour of electrons and hydrogen atoms, but was found to also describe particles with negative energies. It must have been tempting for Dirac to simply dismiss such solutions as "non-physical"; however, strange things are known to occur in quantum mechanics, and intuitions about what is "non-physical" are not so clear. So Dirac investigated the possibility of negative energy solutions and, in particular, to give an account of why a particle cannot make a transition from a positive energy state to a negative one.

Dirac realised that the Pauli exclusion principle would prevent electrons from dropping back to negative energy states if such states were already occupied by negative energy electrons so widespread as to be undetectable. Furthermore, if a negative energy electron was raised to a positive energy state, it would leave behind an unoccupied negative energy state. This unoccupied negative energy state would act like a positively charged electron or a "positron." Thus, Dirac, by his faith in the mathematical part of relativistic quantum mechanics and his reluctance to discard what looked like non-physical solutions, predicted the positron.[31]

This story is even more remarkable for the fact that Dirac was trying to reconcile quantum mechanics with special relativity by reworking Schrödinger's wave mechanics in terms of particle waves. This point of view is, as we now know, largely mistaken. The proper context for reconciling special relativity and quantum mechanics is via quantum field theory, and yet the mathematical component of Dirac's theory has survived; indeed, it is an important part of modern quantum field theory (Weinberg, 1993, pp. 120–121). So not only did Dirac's equation play a significant role in predicting a novel entity, despite the relevant solutions seeming non-physical, it did so based largely on false assumptions. It is hard to see how a nominalised version of Dirac's theory would have had the same predictive success.[32]

---

[31] The positron was subsequently identified in 1932 as an ingredient of cosmic rays.

[32] I am reminded of a quotation from Richard Feynman here: "When you get it right, it is obviously right ... because usually what happens is that more comes out than goes in" (1965, p. 171). The "something more" here is antimatter.

4.4.3 The Lorentz Transformations

This final example is similar to the previous one in some ways. We will see how a set of equations known as the Lorentz transformations were part of an essay written in 1904 by H. A. Lorentz based on some fairly strange assumptions, and yet these same transformations became an integral part of Einstein's special relativity a year later, based on entirely different assumptions. What's more, the predictions of the equations have since been experimentally verified. So again we see an example of some mathematical equations surviving the death of the theory that spawned them, thus suggesting that the mathematics is capturing something that the original theory did not.

The "luminiferous ether" was postulated by physicists in the middle of the nineteenth century[33] as the medium through which Maxwell's electromagnetic radiation must be transmitted, since a wave propagating through a vacuum seemed altogether too strange. Indeed, even Maxwell seemed to support such a theory (Berstein, 1973, p. 39). Furthermore, it was proposed that this ether may provide the "absolute rest" frame for Newtonian mechanics. Granted these assumptions, it was then reasonable to assume that the earth should be moving relative to the frame of the ether, so we ought to be able to detect an "ether wind" as a result of this motion.

In 1887 Albert Michelson and Edward Morley conducted an ingenious experiment designed to detect the "ether wind." This experiment made use of a piece of equipment known as an interferometer, which consisted of two arms of equal length set at right angles to one another along which two beams of light were "raced." By observing interference patterns (if any) between the two light beams, very small differences in the average velocities (relative to the earth) of the two beams of light could be detected. Indeed, one would expect a difference, since, by elementary physics, the beam of light travelling into the ether wind (and back again) should travel slower than the beam travelling across the ether wind. The fact that no difference was ever detected, despite exacting levels of precision and many repeats of the experiment, was one of the great problems for physicists in the latter part of the nineteenth and the early twentieth centuries.

One explanation for the failure of the Michelson-Morley experiment to detect any such velocity difference was offered by George FitzGerald in 1892. FitzGerald proposed that the arm of the interferometer travelling into the ether was shortened by exactly the amount required for the two light beams to take the same time for their respective journeys. This seemingly ad hoc idea was given support by Lorentz in his 1895 essay; in his

---

[33] The concept of the ether, however, goes back at least as far as Descartes.

1904 essay he offered an explanation for this phenomenon in terms of his theory of electromagnetic forces. In this latter essay, Lorentz gives a mathematical statement of this shortening as a function of the velocity of the interferometer relative to the "stationary frame of reference" of the ether. The resulting equations are now known as the Lorentz transformations. These four equations state that there will be a contraction of the length of the arm of the interferometer travelling into the ether but no corresponding contraction in either of the two directions perpendicular to this, and so, in particular, there will be no shortening of the length of the other arm. The fourth equation was a time-dilation equation. This stated that a clock in motion runs more slowly than a stationary one. Lorentz, however, insisted that there was only one "true" time and that the "local time" introduced was just a mathematical device to simplify Maxwell's equations for bodies in motion—it had no physical significance (Berstein, 1973, pp. 71–79).

It is now well known that these equations are an integral part of special relativity, although in special relativity they are based on much more reasonable assumptions: Namely, the principle of relativity[34] and the principle of constancy[35] (Einstein, 1905, pp. 37–38). In fact, it might be argued that in Einstein's theory the Lorentz transformations are derived by careful attention to what we *mean* by length and time, rather than being motivated by an ad hoc defence of the ether.[36]

The point this example illustrates is that whatever merit Lorentz's theory had, and this merit was quite considerable (since his theory predicted the novel phenomenon of the FitzGerald-Lorentz contraction, among other things), it was surely largely in the transformations themselves, since presumably the underlying theory was false. It is hard to see how a nominalistic version of this theory would have made such predictions, since the predictive success of the theory came from the fact that the extremely abstract nature of mathematics allowed abstraction away from the false underlying principles.[37]

---

[34] The laws of physics are the same for all inertial reference frames.

[35] The speed of light (in a vacuum) is a constant for all inertial reference frames.

[36] I don't mean to denigrate Lorentz's theory; indeed, Lorentz and Henri Poincaré very nearly produced the special theory of relativity between them. In fact, the renowned physicist Sir Edmund Whittaker thought Einstein's role in the formulation of special relativity was overemphasized when he summarised Einstein's contribution in his 1910 book on the history of the theories of the ether and electricity in the single sentence: "Einstein published a paper [the 1905 paper] which set forth the relativity theory of Poincaré and Lorentz with some amplifications, and which attracted much attention" (Bernstein, 1973, p. 72). Needless to say, most physicists did not agree with Whittaker's deflationary account of Einstein's contribution.

[37] To put it another way, there are bridge laws between the mathematised Lorentz theory and the nominalised version of the same but also between the mathematised

4.5   Review of Field's Fictionalism

To sum up, then. I have argued that an entity is dispensable to a theory if a *better* theory can be constructed from the first, in which the entity in question plays no part. Confirmation theory was seen to be important here, in that it provided grounds on which to base decisions about which of two competing theories is the better. Hence, confirmation theory plays a crucial role in indispensability decisions. Furthermore, it is around this sense of 'dispensable' that Quine's indispensability argument revolves.[38] It follows then that any critic of the indispensability argument who wishes to deny that mathematics is indispensable to our best physical theories is obliged not only to give an account of how scientific theories may be constructed without reference to mathematical entities of any kind, but also to show that the resulting theory is preferable to the original.[39]

While I admit that I have remained rather vague about the details of how to compare theories, nevertheless, I *have* presented a case for accepting that mathematical entities directly contribute toward qualities such as boldness and unificatory power, which we see as properties of good theories. Critics may argue about degrees of unification and boldness and the like, but at the very least they must demonstrate that scientific theory stripped of all its mathematical entities has some degree of virtue comparable to the original theory (if indeed science can be stripped of all its mathematical entities in the first place). It is difficult to see how this could be done given that, in general, we don't understand why it is that mathematics contributes to the virtue of those portions of science that make use of it. In the words of the renowned mathematical physicist Eugene Wigner:

> The miracle of the appropriateness of the language of mathematics
> for the formulation of the laws of physics is a wonderful gift which
> we neither understand nor deserve. (Wigner, 1960, p. 14)

It is perhaps being altogether too unreasonable to expect such a "miracle" of the nominalist's formalisation of science as well. This is not to be taken as a fatal blow to nominalist programs such as Hartry Field's. I merely want

---

Lorentz theory and special relativity.

[38] As far as I know Quine does not explicitly endorse the position I argue for in this chapter. The position I've argued for, however, does sit well with Quine's views about theory choice and the philosophy of science generally. This, then, may be one of the places where my account diverges from the letter of Quine's, but my account is clearly still Quinean in spirit.

[39] John Burgess (1983) argues for a similar conclusion in his discussion of revolutionary nominalism. The difference, though, is that Burgess sees the question of theory choice, between Platonistic and nominalistic scientific theories, as a separate issue from that of indispensability, whereas I see it as part of what we mean by "indispensability."

to point out *what is required of them* in the light of the indispensability argument, something which is all too easily overlooked.

Field himself, however, does seem to recognise at least some of the requirements I have outlined in this chapter. For example, he argues that nominalistic theories can be "more illuminating" than their Platonistic counterparts (Field, 1980, p. 44). He also rejects Craigian reaxiomatisations as a way of showing entities to be dispensable because such axiomatisations are unattractive (Field, 1980, p. 4).[40] Field recognises that it is not enough to show that mathematical entities are eliminable from empirical science—he is also committed to ensuring that the nominalised theories are attractive theories. Indeed, he goes to some trouble to highlight what he takes to be the virtues of the nominalised theories (apart from their being nominalistic, of course). Their principal virtue is, essentially, that they offer intrinsic explanations for certain facts that are non-arbitrary.[41]

I have two points in response to this. First, I wonder if there isn't just a hint of question begging going on when Field claims that the Hilbert explanation is "intrinsic." For if one thinks, as the indispensabilist does, that numbers are real and intimately (although not causally) involved with the way the world works, it is not clear that explanations of features of space that do not involve numbers are any more intrinsic than electron-free explanations of lightning. The point is that if you think nominalism is correct, then nominalist explanations will seem intrinsic while Platonist ones will not. The Platonist need not concede this. Hilbert's explanation is indeed an *illuminating* explanation of a remarkable fact about space, but it is not clear to me that, short of begging the question against the Platonist, it is an *intrinsic* explanation.[42]

My second point is that, while it is clear that this feature of geometric laws *is* given a more illuminating explanation in Hilbert's theory, it must be remembered that it is *only with respect to this feature of geometry* that Hilbert's theory claims some advantage. Why believe that this illumination is anything more than what happens when one views familiar things from

---

[40] Also see his remarks about how to choose between Platonism with a compact, recursively enumerable logic and nominalism with a higher-order logic. Here he tells us that "the methodology to employ in making such decisions is a holist one: we should be guided by considerations of simplicity and attractiveness of overall theory" (Field, 1980, p. 97).

[41] For example, Hilbert's axiomatisation of geometry explains why geometric laws formulated in terms of distance are invariant under multiplication by a positive constant. See section 4.1.2.

[42] For example, according to structuralists such as Resnik (1997) and Shapiro (1997) the natural numbers are progressions of structural positions. It might then be argued that on such a view natural numbers are intrinsic features of space-time since space-time must contain such progressions.

a different viewpoint? For example, the explanation of why the polynomial $X^2 + 1$ has no real roots is seen very clearly by considering the function $f : \mathbb{R} \to \mathbb{R}$ such that $f(x) = x^2 + 1$ and noticing that the graph of the latter does not intersect the x-axis. This explanation is quite enlightening.[43] It is not, however, any reason for thinking that the geometric interpretation is any more important than the algebraic interpretation, for there are various other facts that are more readily explained algebraically.[44] So too with the case in question. Other features of space are given more illuminating explanations in the standard axiomatisation.[45]

Where does all this leave us then? Field accepts that it is not enough to eliminate mathematical entities from our best scientific theories: The resulting theories must be attractive. I have argued that the resulting theories must, in fact, be more attractive (or at least *as* attractive)—a small point, but worth bearing in mind. In light of this, Field draws attention to a feature of his nominalised theories that he sees as a point in their favour. I have also drawn attention to some desirable features of the Platonistic theories that seem hard to reproduce without mathematical entities. It appears we're left with a rather unsatisfying stand-off. Indeed, it is hard for either side of this debate to do any better at this time. It's difficult enough to compare the virtues of two theories when they are both available for scrutiny, but in this case, the comparison is near impossible, since the nominalist theories in question are not yet available. This fact, along with the worries mentioned earlier (in section 4.1.2) about whether Field's program can be successfully completed, suggests that the Quinean indispensabilist is entitled to wait and see how much of science Field's program can nominalise and how attractive the resulting theories are. I suspect that even if Field's program can be completed for sufficiently large portions of current science, the resulting theories will lack the required degree of virtue for it to be said that mathematical entities have been shown to be dispensable, but this is just a hunch—we must wait and see. In the meantime, I take it that the indispensability argument stands, since the burden of proof in this debate lies with Field, and despite his impressive efforts thus far, he has not yet discharged this burden.

Although I am not yet convinced that Field's program will be successful, I have no doubt about the importance of his program. Indeed, I, like Field, believe that the correct philosophical stance with regard to the realism/anti-realism debate in mathematics hangs on the outcome of

---

[43] Indeed, that this and other such explanations are so enlightening accounts for the importance of Descartes' great insight into the relationship between geometry and algebra.

[44] Such as the fundamental theorem of algebra.

[45] Such as the triangle inequality.

his program. However, not everyone takes this view. In the next chapter I turn to some criticisms of the indispensability argument from Penelope Maddy, which are in some ways more fundamental than Field's. Maddy disagrees that the indispensability argument is a good argument, even if mathematics turns out to be indispensable to science. If she is right about this, then Field's program is irrelevant to whether mathematical objects ought to be considered real or not (Maddy, 1996b, pp. 67–68).

5

Maddy's Objections

In a series of recent essays,[1] one-time mathematical realist Penelope Maddy has presented some serious objections to the indispensability argument. Indeed, so serious are these objections, that she has renounced the realism she so enthusiastically argued for in Maddy (1990a).[2] That realism depended crucially on indispensability arguments. Although her objections to indispensability arguments are largely independent of one another, there is a common thread that runs through each of them. Maddy's arguments draw attention to problems of reconciling the naturalism and confirmational holism required for the Quine/Putnam indispensability argument. In particular, she points out how a holistic view of scientific theories has problems explaining the legitimacy of certain aspects of scientific and mathematical practices—practices that presumably *ought to be* legitimate given the high regard for scientific methodology that naturalism endorses.

5.1 The Objections

5.1.1 The Scientific Fictions Objection

The first objection to the indispensability argument, and in particular to confirmational holism, is that the actual attitudes of working scientists toward the components of well-confirmed theories vary "from belief to grudging tolerance to outright rejection" (Maddy, 1992, p. 280). In "Taking

---

[1] See Maddy (1992; 1995; 1996c; 1998b).

[2] She implicitly renounces the set theoretic realism of *Realism in Mathematics* in many places, but she explicit renounces it in her latest book (Maddy (1997)).

Naturalism Seriously" Maddy (1994) presents a detailed and concrete example that illustrates these various attitudes. The example is the history of atomic theory from early last century, when the (modern) theory was first introduced, until early this century, when atoms were finally universally accepted as real. The puzzle for the Quinean "is to distinguish between the situation in 1860, when the atom became 'the fundamental unit of chemistry', and that in 1913, when it was accepted as real" (Maddy, 1994, p. 394). After all, if the Quinean ontic thesis is correct, then scientists ought to have accepted atoms as real once they became indispensable to their theories (presumably around 1860), and yet renowned scientists such as Poincaré and Ostwald remained sceptical of the reality of atoms until as late as 1904.

For Maddy the moral to be drawn from this episode in the history of science is that "the scientist's attitude toward contemporary scientific practice is rarely so simple as uniform belief in some overall theory" (Maddy, 1994, p. 395). Furthermore, she claims that "[s]ome philosophers might be tempted to discount this behavior of actual scientists on the grounds that experimental confirmation is enough, but such a move is not open to the naturalist" (Maddy, 1992, p. 281), presumably because "naturalism counsels us to second the ontological conclusions of natural science" (Maddy, 1995, p. 251). She concludes:

> If we remain true to our naturalistic principles, we must allow a distinction to be drawn between parts of a theory that are true and parts that are merely useful. We must even allow that the merely useful parts might in fact be indispensable, in the sense that no equally good theory of the same phenomena does without them. Granting all this, the indispensability of mathematics in well-confirmed scientific theories no longer serves to establish its truth. (Maddy, 1992, p. 281)

I will not discuss my reply to this or any other of her objections until I present them all, since at least some of my remarks will apply to more than one of them.

5.1.2   The Role of Mathematics in Science

The next problem for indispensability that Maddy suggests follows on from the last. Once one rejects the picture of a scientific theory as a homogeneous unit, there's a need to address the question of whether the mathematical portions of theories fall within the true elements of the confirmed theories. To answer this question, Maddy points out first that much mathematics is used in theories that make use of hypotheses that are explicitly false, such as the assumption that water is infinitely deep in the analysis of water waves or that matter is continuous in fluid dynamics. Furthermore, she argues that these hypotheses are indispensable to the relevant theory, since the theory would be unworkable without them. It would be foolish, however, to argue for the reality of the infinite simply because it appears in our best theory of water waves (Maddy, 1995, p. 254).

Next she looks at instances of mathematics appearing in theories not known to contain explicitly false simplifying assumptions and she claims that "[s]cientists seem willing to use strong mathematics whenever it is useful or convenient to do so, without regard to the addition of new *abstracta* to their ontologies, and indeed, even more surprisingly, without regard to the additional physical structure presupposed by that mathematics" (Maddy, 1995, p. 255). In support of this claim she looks at the use of continuum mathematics in physics. It seems the real numbers are used purely for convenience. No regard is given to the addition of uncountably many extra entities (from the rationals, say) or to the seemingly important question of whether space and time (which the reals are frequently used to model) are in fact continuous or even dense. Nor is anyone interested in devising experiments to test the density or continuity of space and time. She concludes that "[t]his strongly suggests that *abstracta* and mathematically-induced structural assumptions are not, after all, on an epistemic par with physical hypotheses" (Maddy, 1995, p. 256).

5.1.3 The Mathematical Practice Objection

Maddy begins this objection by noting what she takes to be an anomaly in Quinean naturalism, namely, that it seems to respect the methodology of empirical science but not that of mathematics. It seems that, by the indispensability argument, mathematical ontology is legitimised only insofar as it is useful to empirical science. This, claims Maddy, is at odds with actual mathematical practice, where theorems of mathematics are believed because they are proved from the relevant axioms, *not* because such theorems are useful in applications (Maddy, 1992, p. 279). Furthermore, she claims that such a "simple" indispensability argument leaves too much mathematics unaccounted for. Any mathematics that does not find applications in empirical science is apparently without ontological commitment. Quine himself suggests that we need some unapplied mathematics in order to provide a simplificatory rounding out of the mathematics that is applied, but "[m]agnitudes in excess of such demands, e.g. $\beth_\omega$ or inaccessible numbers"[3] should be looked upon as "mathematical recreation and without ontological rights" (Quine, 1986, p. 400).[4]

Maddy claims that this is a mistake, as it is at odds with Quine's own naturalism. Quine is suggesting we reject some portions of accepted mathematical theory on non-mathematical grounds. Instead, she suggests the following modified indispensability argument:[5]

> [T]he successful application of mathematics gives us good reason to believe that there are mathematical things. Then, given that mathematical things exist, we ask: By what methods can we best determine precisely what mathematical things there are and what properties these things enjoy? To this, our experience to date resoundingly answers: by mathematical methods, the very methods mathematicians use; these methods have effectively produced all

---

[3] $\beth_\omega = \bigcup_{\alpha \in \omega} \beth_\alpha$, where $\beth_\alpha = 2^{\beth_{\alpha-1}}$, α is an ordinal and $\beth_0 = \aleph_0$. See Enderton (1977, pp. 214–215) for further details.

A cardinal number κ is said to be inaccessible iff the following conditions hold: (a) $\kappa >$ $\aleph_0$ (some texts omit this condition) (b) $\forall \lambda < \kappa$ $2^\lambda < \kappa$ and (c) It is not possible to represent κ as the supremum of fewer than κ smaller ordinals (i.e., κ is *regular*). For example, $\beth_\omega$ satisfies (a) and (b) but not (c). $\aleph_0$ satisfies (b) and (c) but obviously not (a). Inaccessible numbers have to be postulated (by large cardinal axioms) in much the same way as the axiom of infinity postulates (a set of cardinality) $\aleph_0$.

[4] More recently Quine has refined his position on the higher reaches of set theory and other parts of mathematics, which are not, nor are ever likely to be, applicable to natural science. For instance, in his most recent book, he suggests:

> They are couched in the same vocabulary and grammar as applicable mathematics, so we cannot simply dismiss them as gibberish, unless by imposing an absurdly awkward gerrymandering of our grammar. Tolerating them, then, we are faced with the question of their truth or falsehood. Many of these sentences can be dealt with by the laws that hold for applicable mathematics. Cases arise, however (notably the axiom of choice and the continuum hypothesis), that are demonstrably independent of prior theory. It seems natural at this point to follow the same maxim that natural scientists habitually follow in framing new hypotheses, namely, simplicity: economy of structure and ontology. (Quine, 1995, p. 56)

A little later, after considering the possibility of declaring such sentences meaningful but neither true nor false, he suggests:

> I see nothing for it but to make our peace with this situation. We may simply concede that every statement in our language is true or false, but recognize that in these cases the choice between truth and falsity is indifferent both to our working conceptual apparatus and to nature as reflected in observation categoricals. Quine, 1995, p. 57)

Elsewhere (1992, pp. 94–95) he expresses similar sentiments.

[5] This suggestion was in fact made earlier by Hartry Field (1980, pp. 4–5), but of course he denies that any portion of mathematics is indispensable to science so he had no reason to develop the idea.

of mathematics, including the part so far applied in physical science. (Maddy, 1992, p. 280)

This modified indispensability argument and, in particular, the respect it
pays to mathematical practice, she finds more in keeping with the spirit, if
not the letter, of Quinean naturalism.

She then goes on to consider how this modified indispensability argument squares with mathematical practice. She is particularly interested in
some of the independent questions of set theory such as Cantor's famous
continuum hypothesis: Does $2^{\aleph_0} = \aleph_1$? and the question of the Lebesgue
measurability of Σ_2^1 sets.[6] One aspect of mathematical realism that Maddy
finds appealing is that independent questions such as these ought to have
determinate answers, despite their independence from the usual ZFC axioms. The problem though, for indispensability-motivated mathematical
realism, is that it is hard to make sense of what working mathematicians
are doing when they try to settle such questions, or so Maddy claims.

For example, in order to settle the question of the Lebesgue measurability of the Σ_2^1 sets, new axioms have been proposed as supplements to
the standard ZFC axioms. Two of these competing axiom candidates are
Gödel's axiom of constructibility, $V = L$, and some large cardinal axiom,
such as MC (there exists a measurable cardinal). These two candidates
both settle the question at hand, but with different answers. MC implies
that all Σ_2^1 sets are Lebesgue measurable, whereas $V = L$ implies that there
exists a non-Lebesgue measurable Σ_2^1 set. The consensus of informed opinion is that $V \neq L$ and that some large cardinal axiom or other is true,[7] but
the reasons for this verdict seem to have nothing to do with applications
in physical science. Indeed, much of the appeal of large cardinal axioms is
that they are less restrictive than $V = L$, so to oppose such axioms would
be "mathematically counterproductive" (Maddy, 1995, p. 265). These are
clearly intra-mathematical arguments that make no appeal to applications.

Furthermore, if indispensability theory is correct, it is quite possible that
physical theories would have some bearing on developments in set theory,
since they are both part of the same overall theory. For example, Maddy

---

[6] Σ_2^1 sets are part of the projective hierarchy of sets, obtained by repeated operations
of projection and complementation on open sets. The Σ_2^1 sets, in particular, are obtained
from the open sets (denoted Σ_0^1) by taking complements to obtain the Π_0^1 sets, taking
projections of these to obtain the Σ_1^1 sets, taking complements of these to obtain the
Π_1^1 sets and finally, taking the projections of these to obtain the Σ_2^1 sets. See (Maddy,
1990a, chapter 4) (and references contained therein) for further details and an interesting
discussion of the history of the question of the Lebesgue measurability of these sets.

[7] There are, of course, some notable supporters of $V = L$, in particular, Quine (1992,
p. 95) and Devlin (1977).

claims that if space-time is not continuous, as some physicists are suggesting,[8] this would undermine much of the need for set theory (at least in
contexts where it is interpreted literally) beyond cardinality $\aleph_0$. Questions
about the existence of large cardinals would be harder to answer in the positive if it seemed that indispensability considerations failed to deliver cardi-
nalities as low as $\beth_1$. Maddy thus suggests that indispensability-motivated
mathematical realism advocates set theorists looking at developments in
physics (theories of quantum gravity in particular) in order to tailor set
theory to best accord with such developments.[9] Given that set theorists in
general do not do this, a serious revision of mathematical practice is being
advocated by indispensability theory, and this, Maddy claims, is a violation
of naturalism (1992, p. 289). She concludes:

> In short, legitimate choice of method in the foundations of set theory
> does not seem to depend on physical facts in the way indispensability
> theory requires. (Maddy, 1992, p. 289)

I'll now defend the indispensability argument against Maddy's three
objections. Before I address each objection, though, it will be useful to
examine Maddy's conception of naturalism a little closer, as my reply to
her objections depends on a clear understanding of her naturalism. Indeed,
I believe that there has been a certain amount of confusion over how naturalism is to be understood in the context of the indispensability argument,
and this confusion has allowed her objections to seem more damaging than
perhaps they ought.

5.2   Maddy's Naturalism

It might be argued that there are two ways in which Maddy's conception
of naturalism differs from Quine's. The first she points out herself:

> On this view [Quinean naturalism], the philosopher occupies no priv-
> ileged position from which to critique the practice of natural science;
> if philosophy conflicts with that practice, it is the philosophy that
> must give. As a philosopher of mathematics, I extend this com-
> pliment to the practice of classical mathematics as well. (Maddy,
> 1998a, p. 176)

She then remarks in a footnote that "[i]t isn't clear that Quine would ap-
prove this extension" (Maddy, 1998a, p. 176). The result of this extension is

---

[8] For example, Richard Feynman (1965, pp. 166–167) suggests this.

[9] Cf. Chihara (1990, p. 15) for similar sentiments.

her modified indispensability argument, which I discussed in section 5.1.3. Recall that Maddy finds Quine's rejection of quantities such as $\beth_\omega$ against the spirit of naturalism, since accepted mathematical practice is rejected on non-mathematical grounds. I shall discuss this departure from Quinean naturalism in more detail when I come to defend the indispensability argument against the mathematical practice objection. At this stage I merely wish to point out that there *is* a departure and that Maddy recognises this.

The other way in which Maddy's naturalism might be thought to differ from Quinean naturalism is also illustrated in the passage just cited. It is seen in the move from "the philosopher occupies no privileged position" to "if philosophy conflicts with [scientific] practice, it is the philosophy that must give." Surely the former does not imply the latter. Quinean naturalism tells us that there is no supra-scientific tribunal, whereas Maddy seems to be suggesting that this implies science itself is in a privileged position. That is, the philosopher of science must merely rubber-stamp *any* scientific practice. Elsewhere she echoes this view of naturalism. For example, in "Set Theoretic Naturalism" she writes, "the [set theory] methodologist's job is to account for set theory as it is practiced, not as some philosophy would have it be" (Maddy, 1996a, p. 490).

There is much ground between a first philosophy, which Quine rejects, and the rubber-stamp role, which Maddy seems to advocate. For instance, there is the position that science and philosophy are continuous with one another and as such there is *no* high court of appeal. On this view, the philosopher of science has much to contribute to discussions of both scientific methodology and ontological conclusions, as does the scientific community. It may be that you're inclined to give more credence to the views of the scientific community in the eventuality of disagreement between scientists and philosophers, but even this does not imply that it is philosophy that must always give. I take it that this view of science and philosophy as continuous, without either having the role of "high court," is in fact the view that Quine intends. It seems that Maddy's interpretation of naturalism represents a significant departure from this view.

Unfortunately things are not that simple, for Maddy also points out that on her view of naturalism "[c]urrent scientific practice need not be taken as gospel, but as a starting point, as prima facie gospel only, subject to ordinary scientific critique" (Maddy, 1998a, p. 178). She then goes on to consider the role of the philosopher:

> How ... does the philosophical methodologist differ from any other scientist? If she uses the same methods to speak to the same issues, what need is there for philosophers at all? The answer, I think, is that philosophical methodologists differ from ordinary scientists

> in training and perspective, not in the evidential standards at their
> disposal. (Maddy, 1998a, p. 178)

The view expressed in these quotations seems at odds with the previous
picture of Maddy's naturalism. In particular, the role of the philosopher
suggested in the last passage is decidedly different to the powerless bureau-
crat rubber-stamping any scientific practice. I have no quarrel with Maddy
on the account of naturalism suggested in these passages.

Which view does she take then? Is it always philosophy that must give or
can philosophers participate as equals in debates on scientific methodology?
Before answering these questions I think it's important to emphasize that
Maddy's claim is that naturalism implies that in the event of a dispute
between philosophy and scientific practice it is *philosophy* that must give,
not *philosophers* that must give. She, like Quine, is against first philosophy
no matter who the practitioners are, scientists, philosophers, or anyone else.
She is careful to point out that the naturalistic enterprise must separate the
good philosophy (i.e., the philosophy that is continuous with science) from
the bad philosophy (i.e., the first philosophy) and that this is a very difficult
enterprise (Maddy, 1995, p. 261). So perhaps rather than "philosophy must
give" she really just means *first* philosophy must give. No doubt Quine
would agree with the latter but, as I've already suggested, not the former.

Although in Maddy's writings it is not always clear which of the two
formulations of naturalism she endorses, I take it that she does in fact
endorse the standard Quinean position of rejecting first philosophy (not
all philosophy). My evidence for this is in part passages such as the ones
just cited where she is clearly more careful about stating her position, and
in part private communication with Maddy on the matter. So Maddy's
naturalism departs from Quine's in only the first way (i.e., she extends
naturalism to endorse the practice of classical mathematics), but we must be
careful, for she sometimes writes as though she departs in the second way as
well (i.e., to endorse the "philosophy must give" formulation of naturalism).
As we shall see in the next section, both these points are important when
considering her objections to the indispensability argument.

5.3 Defending the Indispensability Argument

In this section I will reconsider the three objections to the indispensability
argument raised in section 5.1.

5.3.1 The Scientific Fictions Objection Revisited

Recall that this objection draws attention to the fact that scientists themselves distinguish between the real and the fictional entities in scientific theories. There are two cases to be considered here. The first is the case of scientific fictions that are clearly intended as fictions. I have in mind here such entities as frictionless planes, inertial reference frames, and incompressible fluids. There are a number of reasons for such entities to be taken to be fictional. One reason is that typically the presumed existence of such entities renders inconsistent either the theory in which they occur or another related theory.[10] Given that consistency is one of the more important virtues of scientific theories, any entity that renders the best available theory inconsistent is unlikely to be indispensable to that theory (no matter how useful it is) because there exists a better theory (i.e., a consistent theory) that does not quantify over the entity in question.[11]

The second case is more problematic. Here we have some entity, such as the mid-nineteenth-century atom, which was indispensable to the best available theory, and yet many working scientists of the time treated it instrumentally. Maddy takes this to be a problem for Quinean naturalism, since the naturalistic philosopher of science must "second the ontological conclusions of natural science" (Maddy, 1995, p. 251). Here she writes as though naturalism prohibits *any* philosophical critique of scientific methodology, but, as we saw in the previous section, this is a mistake; this is not the way Maddy understands naturalism. Once this misconception is cleared up, we see that the door is open for a critique of the sceptical scientists from a philosophical perspective located *within* the scientific enterprise. The naturalistic philosopher can point to what Putnam (1971, p. 347) calls the "intellectual dishonesty" of using atoms, say, in our best chemical theories, then denying the existence of these very same atoms. This is not to say that the philosopher occupies any privileged position in this debate, but

[10] For Quine's own treatment of such cases (which differs from that presented here) see Quine (1960, pp. 248–251). Also Jody Azzouni (1997a, section 2) gives a nice account of fictional entities of science.

[11] Strictly speaking, the assertion of the existence of a single entity doesn't render the relevant theory inconsistent. It is the conjunction of that sentence and the rest of the theory that is inconsistent; however, we can quite rightly place the blame on a single sentence (or existence statement) in certain circumstances. Consider the example of the frictionless plane. Appeal to frictionless planes simply makes the statement of certain laws of mechanics easier, so omitting such appeals makes little difference to the overall theory. On the other hand, to assert the existence of frictionless planes would require a great deal of modification to existing theory to explain how such an entity as a frictionless plane would be possible, given our current understanding of frictional forces. So, to be more precise, and in keeping with what I've said in chapter 4, I should say that frictionless planes are *dispensable* to the theory of mechanics.

neither is she or he without power.[12]

It may be that scientists such as Poincaré, who were reluctant to believe in the existence of atoms, were being unduly influenced by some non-naturalistic philosophy (such as verificationism). Here the role of the (naturalistic) philosopher of science is clear: try to convince the scientists in question of the benefits of naturalism and of the consequences for the matter at hand. Again I stress that there is no first philosophy in this strategy; just the fair interplay of ideas, as one would expect in the holistic, naturalistic, Quinean vision of science.[13]

From what I've said so far, it seems that the Quinean must think that those scientists refusing to believe in atoms prior to 1904 were doing something wrong. Maddy obviously disagrees; she thinks that these scientists were right and that something is wrong with the Quinean position. The crux of this objection, then, seems to rest on which way your intuitions go on this and other such episodes in the history of science. I'm inclined to think that the scientists in question *were* wrong in this case, but I appreciate that many would not share my intuitions here, so let me investigate briefly other possible responses the Quinean might make.[14]

One alternative is to deny that atoms were indispensable to science prior to 1904; however, this seems unpromising. Another is to consider the possibility of the Quinean ontic thesis applying only to cases where the theory in question is well accepted among the scientific community. The suggestion is simply that in cases where the best theory is controversial, for whatever reasons, one may suspend judgment on the ontological commitments of the theory. Similarly, one might think that ontological commitment is not an all or nothing affair—we could have degrees of belief in theories and, in particular, to the ontological commitments of those theories.[15] If this is correct

[12] One way this response may be blocked is to insist on the "philosophy must give" reading of naturalism discussed in the last section. While I agree that such a reading of naturalism would block the response of this paragraph, it is not Quine's intended reading of naturalism, and the point of Maddy's objection is to demonstrate a tension within the *Quinean* position.

[13] In fact, I think that those scientists who treated the atomic hypothesis instrumentally were adhering to verificationist philosophical principles. One wonders whether a similar incident could occur now in less verificationist times—I suspect not.

[14] It is also worth noting explicitly that since there was substantial disagreement among the scientific community about the ontological status of atoms prior to 1904, and since Maddy clearly endorses Ostwald's and Poincaré's scepticism about such atoms, it seems she must think that those scientists who accepted atoms as real were in the wrong. Thus, I am not alone in opposing some portion of the scientific community on this issue. The real question is not: Who is at odds with the scientific community? but rather: Which portion of the scientific community (if any) do you side with?

[15] You might think that a confirmational holist is committed to belief or disbelief in whole theories, so that differential degrees of belief in parts of theories is not an option.

then we have two alternatives: (1) the controversy over atomic theory at the time gives us good reason to think that prior to 1913 chemistry/atomic theory was in a crisis period and thus the Quinean could suspend judgment on the ontological commitments of the theory (indeed, this may be all that Ostwald and Poincaré were doing), (2) one could argue that given the evidence at the time it would be unwise to give total commitment to either the existence or the non-existence of atoms—some degree of belief strictly between zero and one would be appropriate. (Again Ostwald and Poincaré's insistence on more evidence could be taken to be nothing more than this.) While I won't pursue these two alternatives any further here, they do seem like promising replies to the Maddy objection.

One other point worth noting, before moving on, is that the Quinean picture of science is not necessarily intended to be in accordance with every episode in the history of science. Presumably science can go wrong, and when it does, it will not accord with the Quinean picture. Recall, from section 2.2, that Quinean naturalism is, in part, a normative doctrine about how we ought to decide our ontological commitments; it is not purely descriptive. This is not to say that Maddy's example of nineteenth-century atomic theory is a case where science went wrong. On the contrary, I think some scepticism toward novel entities such as atoms is a healthy part of the scientific method.

5.3.2   The Role of Mathematics in Science Revisited

Recall that this is the objection that scientists seem willing to use whatever mathematics is required, without regard to ontic commitment. Given my remarks on Maddy's naturalism and my consequent reply to the scientific fictions objections, my reply to this objection is predictable, I think. First, I claim that in cases where mathematics is used in blatantly false hypotheses, such as infinitely deep water in physical theories of waves, we need draw no ontological conclusions from the mathematics used, since the theory as a whole is not taken to be literally true. Maddy and I agree thus far.[16] Furthermore, I suggest that there is no essential difference between

---

This is not the case though. Even a confirmational holist such as Quine must decide which parts of a disconfirmed theory are to be rejected and which are to be retained. Such decisions are made by appeal to pragmatic considerations such as simplicity. It seems plausible, at least in the case of a disconfirmed theory, that one's degrees of belief may vary across the theory in question.

[16] According to Michael Resnik's "pragmatic indispensability argument" (see section 1.2.3), the truth of mathematics is presupposed when doing science, even when the scientific theory in which it is being used is false (and even if it is *known* to be false). His argument thus avoids this objection. Although I have some sympathy with this view, for the sake of this discussion at least, I will take the less controversial line of drawing

these cases and the case of a physicist using a strong mathematical theory, which carries with it certain physical assumptions (such as that space-time is continuous). We no more accept that space-time is continuous because of our use of the reals to model it than we believe that our oceans are infinitely deep because this assumption is sometimes necessary when describing waves. The only difference here is that the latter is clearly false while the former is an open question.

What of the mathematics that appears in theories believed to be true? Here Maddy suggests that the naturalistic philosopher must endorse the view of working scientists, which is simply to use whatever mathematics is convenient, without regard for its apparent ontological commitment and, in particular, without affirming the existence of the entities they are using. As in the previous section, I simply deny that naturalistic philosophers must endorse such apparently dishonest behaviour. I am not suggesting that the naturalistic philosopher need be so heavy-handed as to attract the charge of "practising first philosophy," but nonetheless such a philosopher is not without the power to enter into debate with such scientists about their alleged metaphysical dishonesty.[17]

Furthermore, it is not clear that this *is* the attitude working scientists have toward the mathematics they use. In "Naturalism and Ontology" (1995) Maddy cites Richard Feynman's use of real analysis to describe motion, despite his misgivings about the continuity of space and time.[18] While it is clear that Feynman is using real analysis because it is convenient, it is not clear that he is doing so without regard for the ontological commitments. After all, real analysis is ubiquitous in modern physics, so perhaps Feynman is thinking that whatever ontological load comes with the use of real analysis is already being carried. Then, given that real analysis *would* be convenient to use in describing motion, there seems no reason not to use it.[19] Contrast this with the controversy surrounding the *first* usage of

---

ontological conclusions only from theories believed to be true.

[17] Certainly the portrayal of the difference between first philosophy and continuous philosophy as a matter of being "heavy-handed" or not is a bit of a caricature, but like many caricatures there is some truth in it. First philosophy is unwilling to compromise; continuous philosophy is willing to compromise. In any case, I suspect that we can do no better than such vague characterisations. Whether first philosophy is afoot is determined on a case-by-case basis and by careful attention to the details of the cases. On this Maddy clearly agrees.

[18] The Feynman work she refers to is Feynman et al. (1963).

[19] This might seem implausible, since surely the description of motion was one of the first uses of real analysis, so to represent it as I have here is anachronistic. Be that as it may, but Feynman is presenting the material in an undergraduate physics textbook *as though* this were the first time that real analysis had been put to such a use; he does not present it as the first use of real analysis.

calculus in the seventeenth century.

My claim, then, is that scientists don't worry too much about the ontological commitments of some mathematical theory, if that theory is already widely used (such as in Maddy's Feynman example). On the other hand, when some *novel* mathematical theory or entities are introduced, it seems that scientists do worry about the mathematics in question. As I've already suggested, the earliest usage of calculus and, in particular, infinitesimals, seems a clear example of this. Another, more recent, example is the introduction of the *Dirac delta function* to quantum physics.

In order to get around certain problems (such as differentiating a step function), it was necessary to appeal to a "function," $\delta : \mathbb{R} \to \mathbb{R}$, with the following properties:

$$\delta(x) = 0, \quad \forall x \neq 0,$$
$$\int_{-\infty}^{+\infty} \delta(x) \, dx = 1$$

The delta function, although very useful, is a rather strange entity, and its usage naturally attracted much criticism. Even Dirac, who first introduced the function, was not without some concern:

> [A]lthough an improper function [i.e., a Dirac delta function] does not itself have a well-defined value, when it comes as a factor in an integrand the integral has a well-defined value. In quantum theory, whenever an improper function appears, it will be something which is to be used ultimately in an integrand. Therefore it should be possible to rewrite the theory in a form in which the improper functions appear all through only in integrands. One could then eliminate the improper functions altogether. The use of improper functions thus does not involve any lack of rigour in the theory, but is merely a convenient notation, enabling us to express in a concise form certain relations which we could, if necessary, rewrite in a form not involving improper functions, but only in a cumbersome way which would tend to obscure the argument. (Dirac, 1958, p. 59)

If, as Maddy claims, physicists are inclined to simply use whatever mathematics is required to get the job done, without regard for ontological commitments, why was Dirac so intent on dispelling doubts about the use of his new 'function'?

You might be inclined to think that Dirac's (and others') concerns[20] were entirely concerns about rigour or consistency. Indeed, you might think

---

[20] Dirac's informal argument justifying the use of the delta function went some way

that whenever physicists are concerned about the introduction of new mathematics their only concerns are concerns about rigour or consistency. In that case, Maddy could argue that, while her claim that physicists will use whatever mathematics is required is not quite correct, nonetheless, concerns about ontology never constitute a reason for concern over the legitimacy of a piece of mathematics. Certainly concerns about rigour and consistency played important roles in the initial controversy surrounding both infinitesimals and the delta function. That much is clear. It is less clear that these were the *only* concerns. It would be an interesting exercise to try to disentangle the issues of rigour and ontology in such cases. Fortunately this is not required for the task at hand, as there are other cases where the concerns over the introduction of novel mathematical entities are extremely difficult to interpret as being purely about rigour and/or consistency. The first use of the complex numbers to solve quadratic equations by Cardan, around 1545, springs to mind as a case of a consistent theory over which there was considerable debate.

Unlike the cases of infinitesimals and the Dirac delta function, it appears that it was primarily the unusual nature of the entities concerned that worried those making the earliest use of complex number theory. The controversy was over whether the strange new entity $i = \sqrt{-1}$ was a number. Descartes for one thought not and introduced the term "imaginary" for complex roots of quadratics (Kline, 1972, pp. 253–254). Others who were suspicious of complex numbers included Newton (Kline, 1972, p. 254) and even Euler, who, in 1768–69, claimed that complex numbers "exist only in imagination" (Kline, 1972, p. 594). In particular, Newton's suspicions were seemingly due to the lack of physical significance of complex roots (Kline, 1972, p. 254), nothing to do with rigour. Let me make it clear, though, that I'm not claiming there were *no* concerns about rigour in the debate over the use of complex numbers; it's just that such concerns, if they existed, were secondary to what appear to be ontological concerns.

It is also interesting to note in relation to this case that although complex numbers were used in other areas of mathematics and that work on the algebra of complex numbers continued, despite concerns about their use, often proofs appealing to complex numbers were supplemented with proofs that made no such appeals. It wasn't until Gauss's proof of the fundamental theorem of algebra (in 1799), which made essential reference to complex numbers, and until physical applications for complex function theory were

---

to dispelling those concerns, and certainly the 'function' continued to be used, albeit with reservations. The reservations, however, continued until the mathematical theory of distributions was developed to rigorously justify the delta function's usage. As it turns out, the Dirac delta function is not a function at all; it's a distribution.

developed (also in the latter part of the eighteenth century) that controversy over the usage of complex numbers gradually began to subside (Kline, 1972, p. 595). In both cases applications were important: the former an intra-mathematical application, the latter a physical application.

Whether controversy surrounding the use of novel mathematical entities in physical theories is widespread or not I'm in no position to say, but at least it seems that there are *some* cases where physicists are genuinely suspicious of new mathematical entities. Furthermore, in some of these cases it seems extremely plausible that the concerns were, at least in part, concerns about ontology. In any case, even if physicists *did* use whatever mathematics was required, without regard for ontological considerations, this would not imply that the naturalistic philosopher need simply endorse such behaviour, for reasons I have already made clear.

5.3.3   The Mathematical Practice Objection Revisited

This objection to indispensability arguments I take to be the most serious. Recall that this objection suggests that a mathematical realism motivated by indispensability is inconsistent with current accepted mathematical practice. Before addressing the main point of the objection though, I wish to say a few words about Maddy's modified indispensability argument (see section 5.1.3).

I think Maddy is quite right in claiming that (pure) mathematicians are, by and large, not concerned about the applicability of their mathematics,[21] and that they believe a particular theorem because it has been proved from the axioms, not because it has useful applications. There is still an important question about what this belief amounts to: Does believing a theorem to be true in this context simply mean that if the relevant axioms were true, then the theorem would be true, or does it mean the much stronger claim that there is ontological commitment to all the entities quantified over in statement of the theorem? Let me illustrate with a simple example. If I tell you that Sherlock Holmes is a detective and that all detectives have keen eyes for detail, then you can reasonably infer that Sherlock Holmes has a keen eye for detail. That is, you may conclude that Sherlock Holmes has a keen eye for detail in the first sense (i.e., it's true if the relevant axioms are true), but you may not conclude that Sherlock Holmes has a keen eye for detail in the second sense (i.e., that Sherlock Holmes *exists* and has a

---

[21] Cf. G. H. Hardy's remarks: "It is not possible to justify the life of any genuine professional mathematician on the ground of the 'utility' of his work" (1940, pp. 119–120).

keen eye for detail). I suggest that when mathematicians believe a particular theorem to be true, independent of whether it has applications, they
are speaking in the first sense. Mathematicians believe that the theorem
follows from the relevant axioms but remain agnostic about the ontological
commitments of the theorem (or the axioms).[22] The ontological questions
are answered if and when this particular fragment of mathematical theory
finds its way into empirical science.

In fact, it seems quite right that these two questions ought to be separated in such a way and, moreover, that mathematicians should be largely
unconcerned with the question of ontological commitment (in their working
lives at least). This is no different to other areas of science. Theoretical
physicists may investigate various implications of some given theory without
any regard for the ontological commitments of that theory—the ontological commitments will come later, if the theory is found to be useful in
explaining empirical findings.

Maddy's concerns run a little deeper than this though. She is concerned
that the *methodology* of set theory also depends on how much set theory is
required by physics:

> Set theorists appeal to various sorts of nondemonstrative arguments
> in support of their customary axioms, and these logically imply the
> existence of $\beth_\omega$. Inaccessibles are not guaranteed by the axioms,
> but evidence is cited on their behalf nevertheless. If mathematics
> is understood purely on the basis of the simple indispensability ar-
> gument, these mathematical evidential methods no longer count as
> legitimate supports; what matters is applicability alone. (Maddy,
> 1992, pp. 278–279)

She goes on to suggest that such a conclusion is unacceptable, given her
endorsement of "a brand of naturalism that includes mathematics" (Maddy,
1992, p. 279). Although I have some sympathy with her concern here, such
a critique of the simple Quine/Putnam indispensability argument relies
explicitly on Maddy's version of naturalism. In particular, it relies on
the first departure from Quinean naturalism that I discussed in section 5.2.
Furthermore, this objection cannot be sustained given Quinean naturalism.

This is a rather hollow victory for the Quinean, though, if Maddy's

---

[22] Michael Resnik has pointed out to me that mathematicians *are* concerned with ontological commitment to the extent that they want the mathematical theory in question
to have a model. But this is just to say that they want their theories to be consistent.
Presumably the set of *true* mathematical theories is properly contained by the set of
consistent mathematical theories, so the job of ontology is to decide which of the consistent mathematical theories are true. My claim that mathematicians are agnostic about
ontology is simply the claim that they are largely unconcerned with this task.

brand of naturalism is the more plausible. Fortunately this is not the case. Maddy's naturalism, and its respect for the methodology of mathematics, gains much of its appeal by contrasting it with Quinean naturalism, which allegedly pays little or no respect to purely mathematical methodology. But this portrayal of Quinean naturalism is a gross overstatement. The Quinean can agree with Maddy that naturalism demands respect for mathematical methodology, but that this respect is *earned* by the work mathematics does both within mathematics and, ultimately, in empirical science. Maddy, it seems, is willing to pay respect to the methodology of mathematics for its work in mathematics alone. I have no serious objection to Maddy on this score. Although I'm inclined to prefer the Quinean account, Maddy's is an interesting alternative that deserves attention. My point is simply that Quinean naturalism also legitimates respect for mathematical methodology, and so this cannot be a reason for preferring Maddy's naturalism over Quine's.

As for the charge that the simple indispensability argument leaves too much mathematics unaccounted for (i.e., any mathematics that does not find its way into empirical science), this seems to misrepresent the amount of mathematics that has directly or indirectly found its way into empirical science. On a holistic view of science, even the most abstract reach of mathematics is applicable to empirical science so long as it has applications in some other branch of mathematics, which may in turn have applications in some further branch until eventually one of these find applications in empirical science. Indeed, once put this way it is hard to imagine what part of mathematics could possibly be unapplied.[23]

Still I concede that there may be such areas: perhaps as Quine suggests, inaccessible numbers.[24] According to the indispensability argument then, these remote reaches of mathematics are without ontological commitment, so again this seems to me to be right. Maddy's alternative of endorsing ontic commitment to all mathematical entities just because they were arrived at by mathematical methods seems misguided. Mathematicians must be free to investigate possible axiom systems, for instance, without being committed to all the resulting entities.[25] There must be room for what Quine calls "mathematical recreation,"[26] for otherwise it starts to look as

---

[23] Whether these more abstract reaches can be considered indispensable to empirical science is another matter. All I'm claiming here is that these higher reaches are not ignored by the indispensability argument.

[24] Even this may be a bad choice of example, for at least some think that such numbers are not only the best way of rounding out set theory, but also of rounding out our physical theories. This view is at least hinted at by Martin (1998).

[25] Indeed, some of the systems might turn out to be inconsistent.

[26] As Maddy has pointed out to me, there is nothing in her account that explicitly

though the simple act of a mathematician thinking of some entity implies that such entities exist, and such a position, if not outright absurd, faces serious epistemological problems.[27] In short, I reject Maddy's modified indispensability argument. I think the original Quine/Putnam argument gives a perfectly adequate account of mathematics as practised.

Now to the mathematical practice objection. Maddy begins this objection by claiming that a mathematical realist must agree that there is a fact of the matter about the truth values of such independent hypotheses as the continuum hypothesis and the measurability of Σ_2^1 sets. Clearly from what I've said already, I think that for some statements we may refrain from assigning truth values: in particular, to those in areas of mathematics we consider part of mathematical recreation.[28] This, however, clearly does not apply to the questions that Maddy is interested in. These are questions about sets of real numbers and, as I've mentioned previously, real analysis is ubiquitous in natural science and so, by indispensability theory, has as great a claim to real status as any portion of scientific theory.

So is it correct that a realist about some class of entity should agree that every statement about the entities in question is either true or false? It seems not. Many scientific realists would be inclined to dismiss statements about the simultaneous *exact* locations and momenta of fundamental particles as neither true nor false. Can the mathematical realist take a similar line with regard to the truth of the continuum hypothesis, for instance? Although this is a line that some mathematical realists may be inclined to take, I don't find this approach at all appealing. The difference between the scientific realist refusing to assign truth values to statements about the positions and momenta of fundamental particles, and the mathematical realist refusing to assign truth values to any independent statement of mathematics is that in the former case there is a theorem that states exact

---

rules out recreational mathematics. The difference between her and Quine on this point is that for Quine recreational mathematics is marked by its isolation from empirical science, whereas for Maddy it is marked by its differing methodology. For example, the investigation of finite models of arithmetic (see Priest (1997)) will presumably be considered recreational by both Maddy and Quine; by the former because such models are too restrictive and by the latter because they lack the required relationship with empirical science. Thus, we see that on Maddy's account, if a mathematician is using accepted methodology (i.e., doing non-recreational mathematics) to investigate some area of abstract mathematics we must interpret the area of mathematics in question realistically. Again it looks as though the act of mathematical investigation implies the existence of some class of mathematical entities.

[27] Jody Azzouni (1994) defends a position not unlike this.

[28] Although Quine seems to prefer the assignment of truth values in such cases (see footnote 4 of this chapter), this is mainly to avoid the complications of non-bivalent logics (Quine, 1995, p. 57). The difference is not really important here. We might also consider truth to be relative to a model.

limitations on the accuracy of measurements of position and momenta (the Heisenberg uncertainty principle), whereas in the latter case it seems that the refusal to assign truth values is merely to avoid the problem at hand and as such is ad hoc.

Adrian Riskin (1994) argues that the mathematical realist need not accept that there is a fact of the matter about new set-theoretic axioms. He argues that it is quite consistent with Platonism to accept all consistent models of set theory as real, just as most mathematical realists are inclined to think of both Abelian and non-Abelian groups as real. Although I agree with him that such a position is viable and has, as Riskin points out, considerable support from mathematical practice, the claim that all consistent mathematical theories are true is unlikely to receive support from indispensability theory. Recall that the indispensabilist is interested in which of the consistent mathematical theories are required by our best scientific theories and hence deserve to be thought of as true (cf. footnote 22). While it is clear that we require both Abelian and non-Abelian groups in order to do science, it is not so clear that more than one set theory is required. In any case, it seems unlikely that we would require *every* consistent set theory.[29]

So I agree with Maddy that a mathematical realist ought to believe that there is a fact of the matter about answers to independent questions concerning the real numbers (or provide some cogent reason for *not* doing so). It then seems natural that such a realist should also concede that since ZFC is not strong enough to answer such questions, there must be some theory that *is* strong enough, presumably some extension of ZFC. Now Maddy points out

> that this acceptance of the legitimacy of our independent question [Are Σ_2^1 sets Lebesgue measurable?] and ... the legitimacy of its pursuit is not unconditional; it depends on the empirical facts of current science. The resulting mathematical beliefs are likewise a posteriori and fallible. (Maddy, 1992, p. 285)

After considering the implications of the relevant physical theories, namely, quantum gravity, in which the possibility that space-time is discrete arises, she concludes:

> [S]et theorists should be eagerly awaiting the outcomes of debates over quantum gravity, preparing to tailor the practice of set theory to the nature of the resulting applications of continuum mathematics.

[29] Although if an alternative set theory was found to have a model in the accepted set theory (whatever that turns out to be), then Riskin's point can be accommodated without accepting the outright truth of the alternative set theory.

> But this is not the case; set theorists do not regularly keep an eye on developments in fundamental physics. Furthermore, I doubt that the set-theoretic investigation of independent questions would be much affected even if quantum gravity did end up requiring a new and different account of space-time; set theorists would still want to settle open questions about the mathematical continuum. (Maddy, 1992, p. 289)

The first thing to say here is that on the version of the indispensability argument that I endorse (i.e., the original Quine/Putnam argument, *without* Maddy's modification), if there were no use for continuum mathematics anywhere in science (not just as a model of space-time) then a mathematician involved in settling independent questions of real analysis would be pursuing mathematics that has no ontological commitment. That is, she or he would be participating in mathematical recreation. This is not, however, to denigrate such behaviour. Certainly continuum mathematics is an interesting area of mathematics, independent of its applications. In any case, real analysis would certainly still be required as a useful, though dispensable, approximation in many applications. The mathematician working in real analysis would be in the same boat as a modern physicist working on Newtonian mechanics or vacuum solutions to the Einstein equation.

The crux of this objection, then, is to give an account of why set theorists do not keep a close watch on developments in physics in order to help settle the independent questions of set theory. I suggest that this might simply be a case of division of labour. Set theorists do what they do best—set theory! If developments in other areas of science are to have impact on their discipline then most set theorists will not be in a position to properly assess that impact. This is no different from other areas of science, except for the matter of the *scope* of mathematics.

Michael Resnik (1998) suggests that we may construct a rough ranking of the sciences in terms of their scope, in which mathematics is the most global theory since it is presupposed by physics, which in turn is presupposed by chemistry, and so on. Furthermore, this hierarchy imposes certain natural methodological considerations. Anomalies in fairly specialised areas of science, such as molecular biology, are best not resolved by making alterations to more global theories, as alterations in the latter will have ramifications in many other areas of science that will not be foreseen by the molecular biologist. This is nothing more than Quine's Maxim of Minimum Mutilation (Quine, 1992, pp. 14–15) in action.

So we find two reasons for experts not to resolve problems in their own field by proposing changes to another. The first is simply that typically such experts lack the required expertise in the field in which they are proposing the changes. Second, even if they were to possess the required expertise, if the other field were a more global theory than their own, they could not possibly know all the ramifications of such alterations in all the theories that depend on that global theory. Even experts in the more global theory are not in a position to assess such ramifications. This means that scientists working in the most global theories such as mathematics and physics are unlikely to need to revise their theories in light of developments in less global theories. The converse, however, is not true. Scientists working in a particular local theory may need to keep an eye on the relevant global theories to make sure that their work is consistent with those theories.[30]

The relevance of all this to the problem at hand is obvious. Set theorists are working in arguably the most global area of the most global theory. They do not expect to have to modify their theories in light of developments in other areas of science. They are not regularly keeping an eye on less global theories, simply because there is usually no need to do so. On the other hand, it seems that this is a place where the philosopher of mathematics can contribute something. The philosopher of mathematics can keep an eye on developments in other areas of science that may be relevant and assist in the assessment of the importance of those developments and of proposed modifications of current mathematical theory in light of those developments. Of course set theorists would still want to settle the open questions of set theory, regardless of developments in physics, but if such developments meant continuum mathematics had no applications, then set theorists working on the continuum hypothesis, say, would be pursuing mathematical recreation.

5.4 Review of Maddy's Objections

I have considered Maddy's three objections to indispensability arguments and found that in the cases of the objection from scientific fictions (section 5.1.1) and the objection from the role of mathematics in scientific theories (section 5.1.2), much of the force of the objections derived from taking the "philosophy must give" reading of naturalism. This, I argued, was a mistake since neither Quine nor Maddy takes naturalism in this way. On

---

[30] There are, of course, examples where workers in a less global theory continued research in a particular area known to be inconsistent with a relevant global theory. For example, early evolutionary theory required that the earth be much older than pre-atomic physics allowed. That is, pre-atomic physics could not provide a model of the sun emitting energy for the required length of time required for evolution to take place. In this particular case the anomaly was resolved in favour of the biologists, but this does not alter the point that the biologists were painfully aware that evolutionary theory was in tension with the more global theory of physics.

the standard reading of Quinean naturalism, the force of these objections is much reduced, and in both cases more than one solution is possible.

The third of Maddy's objections, the mathematical practice objection (section 5.1.3), was seen to turn on a misconception about Quinean holism. I argued that because a theory is confirmed or disconfirmed as a whole unit does not imply that each fragment of that theory has the same priority. When modification of a theory is required, Quine's Maxim of Minimum Mutilation implores us to modify those areas of the overall theory upon which the least depends. Resnik's global and local distinction was seen to be particularly useful in bringing out this point. The upshot of this is that, given this understanding of holism, once again Maddy's objection cannot be sustained.

Finally, by allowing room for the possibility of mathematical recreation, as does the original Quine/Putnam indispensability argument, we see that mathematicians may pursue research programs that have no direct or indirect application to empirical science and that this accords very well with actual mathematical practice. Furthermore, this feature of indispensability theory is able to explain Maddy's puzzle about why set theorists would want to settle the open questions of set theory, regardless of the applications of such theory: They would be pursuing mathematical recreation.

I should mention one other related issue with which Maddy is interested and which I have not addressed so far in this chapter. The issue concerns the different methodological consequences of a Quinean naturalist's approach to the independent questions of set theory, and Maddy's naturalistic approach. She claims that there are significant differences in the type of justification these two approaches would give for the rejection of $V = L$, for instance. Set theoretic naturalism, as Maddy calls her position, is opposed to this axiom on the grounds that it is too restrictive and that it is desirable to have as rich a set theory as possible. The Quinean naturalist, on the other hand, must give some reason to think that $V = L$ is false. As Maddy rightly points out, "desirability (notoriously!) is no guarantee of truth" (Maddy, 1992, p. 288). The matter is made more complicated by Quine's own preference for $V = L$ over large cardinal axioms on the grounds of ontological parsimony (Quine, 1992, p. 95). Maddy claims, in effect, that Quinean naturalism delivers up $V = L$ and that this is the wrong answer, or at least it's at odds with general consensus. Indeed, Maddy takes this to be a reason to prefer her naturalism over the Quinean variety.[31]

It's not clear, however, that the disagreement over $V = L$ is due to differing conceptions of naturalism; it seems to be more about the different

---

[31] She takes up this issue in *Naturalism in Mathematics* (1997). See also Colyvan (1999a).

weightings of theoretical virtues such as ontological parsimony, unificatory power, elegance, and so on. After all, Quine explicitly gives "considerations of simplicity, economy, and naturalness" as his reasons for preferring $V = L$, because "$[V = L]$ inactivates the more gratuitous flights of higher set theory" (Quine, 1992, p. 95). This seems to have more to do with his well-known taste for desert landscapes than with indispensability considerations. Although the two are closely related in Quine's thinking, it seems that there is room for a defender of the indispensability argument to prefer MC, say, over $V = L$ on the grounds of the unification and expressive power the former brings to science as a whole. The indispensability theorist may well admit that the inflated ontology that MC brings is a cost, but that it is a cost worth incurring. Although such a view is clearly not endorsed by Quine, it is not ruled out by indispensability considerations alone. In short, I think Maddy's quarrel here is with Quine's preference for simplicity, not with the indispensability argument itself.

The related issue of whether Maddy is right or not about her conception of naturalism being preferable to Quine's is also of considerable interest, but is somewhat orthogonal to the main thrust of her objections to the indispensability argument. The important question, for our purposes, is whether *Quinean* naturalism fails to support the indispensability argument. In this chapter I have shown that this question should be answered in the negative.

6

The Empirical Nature of
Mathematical Knowledge

It is generally believed that empirical science provides us with propositions that are a posteriori, contingent and revisable in the light of empirical
evidence. Mathematical propositions, on the other hand, are generally believed to be a priori, necessary and unrevisable in the light of empirical
evidence. But indispensability theory tells us that mathematical knowledge is in the same epistemic boat as empirical knowledge. The tension is
clear, and many authors have exploited this tension, in various ways, to undermine the indispensability argument. In this chapter I will address such
criticisms. In doing so I will be defending the somewhat controversial consequence of the indispensability argument, that mathematical knowledge
has an empirical character.

The idea that mathematics is empirical is certainly not new, nor are
criticisms of such a position. J. S. Mill (1843 [1947]), for example, argued
for an empiricist account of mathematics, and in doing so made himself
the subject of a sustained attack from Frege.[1] Mill took numbers to be
properties of aggregates and arithmetic to be highly general laws of nature
arrived at by observing the behaviour of physical aggregates when adjoined.
Among Frege's complaints was that this was to confuse an application of
arithmetic with arithmetic itself (Dummett, 1991, p. 59). In more recent
times, though, there has been something of a revival of empirical accounts of

---

[1] Frege's arguments against Mill are found in many places but are particularly evident
in his *Die Grundlagen der Arithmetik* part II, section 23 (1884 [1950]).

mathematics.[2] Although many of these accounts have much in common and are of considerable interest, I won't discuss them here, since I am concerned primarily with defending Quine's empirical account of mathematics. That is, mathematical propositions are known a posteriori, because the existence of mathematical objects can be established only by empirical methods—by their indispensable role in our best scientific theories.

In the first section I will address the objection that indispensability theory makes a mystery of the obviousness and clearly a priori character of at least some mathematical knowledge. In the following section I will address an objection from Alan Musgrave that indispensability theory fails to account for the clear difference in modal status between mathematical knowledge and empirical knowledge, the latter being contingent and falsifiable while the former is necessary and unfalsifiable. In the third section I will address Elliott Sober's objection that mathematical theories cannot share the empirical support of our best scientific theories, because mathematics is a common part of *all* such theories. Sober claims that mathematics is not being tested in the same way as the clearly empirical claims of science, and so it cannot be confirmed by the usual empirical methods. Finally I will consider the question of the contingency of mathematical truth and, in particular, I will discuss the debate between Hartry Field and Crispin Wright and Bob Hale.

6.1 The Obviousness of Some Mathematical Truth

Charles Parsons's grievance with indispensability theory is that it doesn't explain the obviousness of so much mathematics (emphasis in original):

> The empiricist view, even in the subtle and complex form it takes in the work of Professor Quine, seems subject to the objection that it leaves unaccounted for precisely the *obviousness* of elementary mathematics (and perhaps also of logic). (Parsons, 1980, p. 101)

According to indispensability theory, mathematical statements such as

There exists an even prime number

or if we formalise this in the obvious way:

$$(\exists x)((Px \& Ex) \& Nx) \tag{6.1}$$

---

[2] See, for example, Lakatos (1976) and Kitcher (1984).

are true by virtue of their role in successful empirical theories. But it seems Parsons is right that (6.1) is just obviously true. We don't need to do any physics or chemistry before we can see that two is prime. Furthermore, Quine's metaphor of mathematics (and logic) being centrally located in the web of belief offers no explanation, since many obvious truths are not centrally located. (I have in mind here obvious truths such as "there are oceans" and the like. These are located near the periphery of the Quinean web—near the boundary conditions of experience.)

It is far from clear, however, that any mathematics is obviously true. After all, Hartry Field and others believe that (6.1) is false, so it can't be all that obvious. It is instructive though, I think, to see why Field believes that (6.1) is false. He doesn't think (6.1) is false because two is odd or because two is composite. He thinks (6.1) is false because *there is no such object as two*. He would agree that the following statement is true:

In the story of number theory there exists an even prime number.

He would also agree to a conditionalised form such as

If number theory is true, then there exists an even prime number.

If we formalise this last statement (again in the obvious way) we obtain:

$$N_T \supset (\exists x)((Px \& Ex) \& Nx). \tag{6.2}$$

Now I claim that (6.2) is obviously true and it is this or something like it[3] that we confuse when we mistakenly agree with Parsons that (6.1) is obviously true. It simply can't be the case that (6.1) is obviously true, for this would mean that the debate over the reality of numbers that has been raging for over two thousand years has an obvious answer—Platonism is correct. Now I'm a Platonist, but I don't think that it is *obvious* that there are numbers.

That we confuse statements such as (6.1) with some other closely related statement such as (6.2) under certain circumstances is not terribly surprising. Usually when asked questions about elementary number theory, we take the context of such questions to be *within* number theory where the answers *are* obvious. Asked the same questions in a metaphysics seminar, the answers cease to be obvious. Furthermore, this phenomenon is not peculiar to mathematics. It's presumably obvious that the following statement is true:

---

[3] Although I think it is (6.2) that is being confused with (6.1), nothing I say here depends on this. All that I require is that there is some statement related to (but not identical with) (6.1) that is obviously true. (6.2) certainly seems like a good candidate.

(*) There is a difference between the political policies of the
Liberals and the Democrats.

It's obviously true in the context of a discussion of Australian politics,
but in the context of a metaphysics debate to admit that (*) is true is
apparently to hold a commitment to the ontological category of *differences*.
Perhaps differences, as an ontological category, do exist, but it's far from
obvious that they do. Nonetheless, there is surely *some* reading of (*) that
is obviously true, and it is this reading, whatever it may be, that we are
confusing with (*) itself when we pronounce (*) obviously true.[4]

I don't wish to belabour what is really quite a simple point, but it
is important to see that what is taken to be obvious does depend in an
important way on context, and the context of the questions that Parsons is
concerned with is that of indispensability theory. This places such questions
squarely in the context of a metaphysics debate where the answers are not
obvious.

I should also point out that there is nothing special about the example
(6.1). You might think that it was the existential quantifier that committed
you to the existence of two in (6.1), and hence the dispute over its truth
value, but this would be a mistake; "$2 + 2 = 4$" would have done just as
well, for surely this, apart from anything else, asserts the existence of two
and four. You might disagree with this Platonistic construal of "$2+2 = 4$."
You might think that it means something like:

> When you take two physical objects (of the right sort) and place
> them next to two other physical objects (of the right sort), you
> have four physical objects.

Or perhaps:

> When I see the marks on the page "$2 + 2$" I know that it is
> permissible to replace such marks with the mark "4."

Such interpretations have existential commitments to physical objects and
marks on pages respectively, but none to numbers. Indeed, some such
interpretation may well be the correct reading of "$2 + 2 = 4$," but it is
certainly not obvious that "$2+2 = 4$" is about marks on a page or physical
objects. It is *apparently* about numbers! Non-Platonistic interpretations
of mathematical propositions, apart from any other problems they face,
are just not obvious and this is all I require here. I happen to agree with
Frege, Quine, Field, and others that statements such as "$2 + 2 = 4$" at
least purport to be about numbers but nothing hangs on this. My claim

---

[4] I'm indebted to Frank Jackson for a useful discussion on this.

is simply that mathematical statements that do not explicitly existentially quantify over mathematical objects, if taken at face value, do, nonetheless, assert that mathematical objects exist. If they are not taken at face value, then it's not obvious what they are about. In either case, they are not *obviously* true.

John Bigelow (in private conversation) has raised a similar concern about the indispensability argument. He points out that mathematics proceeds (apparently) by a priori means and yet, according to indispensability theory, mathematical truths are of the same kind as empirical truths, that is, a posteriori. To use an example of Bigelow's, we don't have to do any empirical investigations to realise that

$$\sum_{j=1}^{n}(2j-1) = n^2. \tag{6.3}$$

Bigelow points out that a Greek mathematician (or anyone untrained in modern science for that matter) could sit down and arrange pebbles to prove this. One simply arranges them thus:[5]

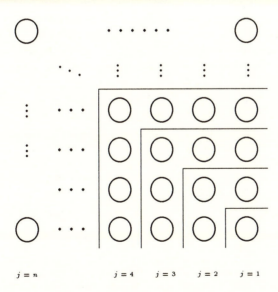

$j = n$ $\qquad$ $j = 4$ $\quad$ $j = 3$ $\quad$ $j = 2$ $\quad$ $j = 1$

Here each Γ-shaped collection of pebbles is called a *gnomon* with the first gnomon ($j = 1$) being the one at the bottom right of the array (i.e., the gnomon with only one pebble), and the others are numbered from right to

---

[5] Bigelow and Pargetter (1990, pp. 350–351) use this example to make a related point.

left. To see how this arrangement proves equation (6.3), one simply needs to see that each gnomon has an odd number of pebbles in it, with gnomon $j = 1$ having one pebble and that each successive gnomon to the left has 2 more pebbles than its predecessor. Moreover, the sum of the pebbles in all the gnomons up to $j = n$ is a square array with n^2 pebbles in it.

Not only is this obvious, it's a priori. On the Quinean account, mathematical statements such as (6.3) are known to be true by the role they play in our best scientific theories—in other words a posteriori. It's interesting to note that in Bigelow's example (6.3) can be quite easily proved using mathematical induction. This too would be an a priori proof, but it would rely on some deeper mathematics, which may in turn rely on further mathematics, which may eventually depend on a posteriori considerations. Indeed, this is typically what the Quinean is inclined to say about such examples. The Bigelow proof, however, doesn't seem to permit such a move, since it doesn't seem to rely on more mathematics—you just "see it." Apart from some quibbles about whether the pebble arrangement really constitutes a proof (which it does not) and whether it implicitly makes use of mathematical induction (which it does), Bigelow's point is a good one.[6]

Before I can address this worry, I need to say something about how we should understand Bigelow's claim that mathematics is a priori. First, we should understand the claim that mathematics is a priori as a claim that we *could* come to know mathematical propositions by a priori means (not as the stronger, and clearly false, claim that we *do*, in general, come to know mathematical propositions by a priori means). Next, we need to come to some understanding of the sense of a priori Bigelow is invoking here, as there are several different ones in the literature.[7] For example, he clearly does not intend the traditional (Kantian) sense, in which a priori knowledge is gained independently of experience, for no matter how you cash out 'experience', gazing at and manipulating pebbles *must* count as experience. Some other accounts of "a priori" on offer are: (1) a priori knowledge is rationally unrevisable; (2) a priori knowledge involves necessity in some way (either as a necessary condition, a sufficient condition or both); or (3) a proposition is a priori if one is justified in believing it once one understands it. I

---

[6] It's worth noting the similarity between Bigelow's objection and the objection raised against Quinean naturalism in section 2.3. Recall that the latter objection was that Quinean naturalism didn't respect a methodological difference between philosophy and science: The former proceeding by a priori methods and the latter by a posteriori methods. In discussing that objection I cast doubt on the viability of maintaining the a priori/a posteriori distinction. I stand by my remarks in that section, but here, for the sake of argument, I grant Bigelow that distinction.

[7] My discussion here follows Albert Casullo's entries "a priori/a posteriori" and "a priori knowledge" in Dancy and Sosa (1992, pp. 1–8).

assume Bigelow does not intend (1), since it is entirely possible that his Greek mathematician revises his or her belief in the truth of (6.3) in the light of new evidence (perhaps another pebble arrangement). I also take it that Bigelow does not intend (2) since it's hard to see how the pebble arrangement is at all relevant to the necessity of (6.3). Instead, I take it that Bigelow is using "a priori" in the third sense. Bigelow's claim then is that the Greek mathematician comes to understand (6.3) via the pebble arrangement and that this is sufficient for him or her to believe (6.3) to be true.[8]

Now to my response to this objection. In short, it is the same as my response to the Parsons objection: I claim that (6.3) is not known a priori. Now it might be that the claims

In the story of number theory $\sum_{j=1}^{n}(2j-1) = n^2$

or

$$N_T \supset \sum_{j=1}^{n}(2j-1) = n^2 \tag{6.4}$$

are known a priori. But it simply cannot be the case that understanding (6.3) is sufficient for believing that integers exist. On the other hand, understanding (6.4) does seem sufficient for believing it to be true. As in the Parsons case, it is these conditional statements (or something like them) that get confused with (6.3).

This confusion is perhaps understandable since, for the most part, when we do elementary mathematics we are not concerned with whether mathematical objects exist or not. A fortiori we are not concerned with how we know whether such objects exist. Still there is the interesting question of why we so often mistakenly believe elementary number theory propositions to be obvious or a priori. One plausible answer is that the confusion arises from the way number theory is learned.

Despite the fact that elementary theorems of number theory are frequently used to demonstrate the alleged a priori nature of mathematical knowledge, I think that number theory is not well suited to this purpose. The reason is that we learn the rudiments of number theory very young and without any concern for ontology. Consequently, when we come to

---

[8] James Chase has pointed out to me that Bigelow's problem can be restated using *any* of these (and perhaps other) senses of a priori. Chase also suggested that this need not concern me too much since, in effect, I deal with the restatements elsewhere. For example, if we take the "rational unrevisability" sense of a priori, the restatement of the Bigelow problem then looks very much like Elliott Sober's objection, which I deal with later in this chapter (section 6.3).

consider examples from number theory in the context of deciding whether mathematics is a priori or a posteriori, our intuitions are corrupted by this deeply ingrained, undiscriminating, early training in arithmetic. For example, when you first come across the Peano axioms, usually at university, they seem obvious, even a priori. To borrow a phrase from Gödel, they "force themselves upon us" (1947, p. 484). Try to imagine never having had any training in mathematics up until that time. Would the Peano axioms still force themselves upon you? I suggest not.

6.2   The Unfalsifiability of Mathematics

Alan Musgrave (1986) has suggested a Popperian worry about the indispensability argument:

> Imagine that all the evidence that induces scientists to believe (tentatively) in electrons had turned out differently. Imagine that electron-theory turned out to be wrong and electrons went the way of phlogiston or the heavenly spheres. Popperians think this *might* happen to any of the theoretical posits of science. But can we imagine natural numbers going the way of phlogiston, can we imagine evidence piling up to the effect that there are no natural numbers? This must be possible, if the indispensability argument is right and natural numbers are a theoretical posit in the same epistemological boat as electrons.

> But surely, if natural numbers do exist, they exist of necessity, in all possible worlds. If so, no empirical evidence concerning the nature of the actual world can tell against them. If so, no empirical evidence can tell in favour of them either. The indispensability argument for natural numbers is mistaken. (Musgrave, 1986, pp. 90–91)

He then discusses this point in relation to Hartry Field's argument from the conservativeness of mathematics. He asks us to assume that mathematics (M) is both consistent and consistent with any (consistent) scientific theory (S):

> [T]hen adding [mathematics] to any scientific theory does not enable us to derive any conclusions about the world that do not follow from the scientific theory alone. (If some conclusion C did follow from M and S which did not follow from S alone, then M would not be consistent with the consistent theory S & not-C.) Hence the truth or falsity of predictions drawn from a scientific theory with the help of a mathematical theory does not really impinge upon the truth or falsity of the mathematical theory. (Musgrave, 1986, p. 91)

Despite the Popperian trappings in the initial formulation of the problem, there is no mention of Popper or falsification in the second. It thus seems that to criticise the Popperian view of science and the concept of falsification,[9] in particular, will not deflect this objection. In any case, I will resist this temptation, since I think there are other faults with this argument. I'll consider the two formulations separately because it turns out that they are quite separate arguments, albeit with a common thread. Let me begin with the first formulation.

The first thing I wish to question about Musgrave's first formulation is the claim that the indispensability argument implies that one must be able to imagine an experiment that will falsify the proposition that there are natural numbers. This is a rather odd way of suggesting that according to indispensability theory mathematical entities are contingent. I don't think that the indispensability argument forces one to this conclusion, although it is a very natural position for an indispensabilist to adopt. But even granting this, it's not clear to me that we ought to be able to imagine an experiment to falsify the claim that there are numbers. Imagination is a very poor guide to what is possible. For instance, it is possible, we now know, to conduct an experiment to falsify the proposition that it is the earth that rotates and not the celestial sphere. This experiment is, of course, Jean Foucault's famous pendulum experiment.[10] But to confuse imaginability with possibility is to rob Foucault of any credit for the ingeniousness of the experiment. In short, even if there is a possible experiment that falsifies some particular proposition, it doesn't follow that we are always able to imagine such an experiment. If this were the case we'd all be great experimental scientists. A fortiori the failure to imagine an experiment to falsify the proposition that there are natural numbers does not imply that there can be no such experiment.

But what if there really is no such experiment? Isn't that Musgrave's point? This would be a problem if it were true, but I believe that there is such an experiment. Suppose that Hartry Field has completed the nominalisation of Newtonian mechanics but that he and his successors repeatedly fail to nominalise general relativity. Let's also suppose that this failure gives us good reason to believe that general relativity cannot be nominalised. From

[9] For instance, see Lakatos (1970), Duhem (1906), and Quine (1951) for criticisms of Popper's falsification principle.

[10] In 1851 Foucault suspended a 60 metre pendulum from the ceiling of the Pantheon in Paris. The pendulum was set in motion and the plane of oscillation was noted, with care being taken to exclude any disturbing forces. Over time the plane of oscillation changed (with respect to the earth), thus providing dramatic and direct confirmation that it was the earth that rotated and not the celestial sphere. See Abell et al. (1987, pp. 89–91) for further details.

this we conclude that mathematical entities are indispensable to general relativity, but not to Newtonian mechanics. In this setting, then, can we imagine an experiment to test the hypothesis that there are natural numbers? The answer is yes. Not only can we imagine such an experiment, we can perform it. In fact many such experiments have been performed over the last 80 years or so, for any experiment that confirms general relativity over Newtonian mechanics is such an experiment. In particular, the 1919 Eddington eclipse experiment is such an experiment.[11]

I take it that Musgrave sees our failure to imagine evidence against the existence of natural numbers to support his claim: "if natural numbers do exist, they exist of necessity" (Musgrave, 1986, p. 91) (for otherwise this important premise is not argued for at all). As we've seen, though, imaginative failure is a poor guide to what is necessary and so the indispensabilist need not accept the idea that numbers exist of necessity. (Indeed, the thoroughgoing Quinean would dismiss the whole notion of necessity!) If all this is correct, then Musgrave's argument collapses. If natural numbers do not exist of necessity, then there *is* evidence that will count for or against them. That evidence comes from the confirmation of our best scientific theories.

Now to the second formulation of his objection. Here Musgrave skips over an important detail of Field's conservativeness argument. Field requires that the scientific theory in question (S) is a *nominalistic* theory, and that the consequences are *nominalistic* consequences (Field, 1980, pp. 7–19). So the conservativeness of mathematics amounts to the claim that no *nominalistic* claim about the world is a consequence of M and S unless it is a consequence of S alone. Musgrave's statement of this argument is either fallacious or question begging. To see this let $C = M$ and assume M doesn't follow from S; then C doesn't follow from S alone, yet it's trivial that C follows from M and S. For Field such cases don't arise because S must be a nominalistic theory and C must be nominalist consequences, so we can't have $C = M$. But Musgrave (1986) describes the consequences as "about the world" (p. 91). That is, either his argument admits the above counterexample or Musgrave takes a proposition being "about the world" to be the same as its being nominalistic. The latter begs the question against the mathematical realist who takes mathematical existence claims to be about the world.

Still, let's grant Musgrave a little charity. Let's suppose that what he means by "about the world" is "about the *physical* world." If this is the case, then it does seem reasonable to suppose his argument is the same as Field's conservativeness argument. But this is not an argument against

---

[11] Colin Cheyne and Charles Pigden (1996) use this example in a slightly different context.

mathematical theories receiving empirical support from the empirical confirmation of our best scientific theories *unless* such theories can be separated into purely mathematical and purely nominalistic components. Such a task is non-trivial. Indeed, Field devotes most of *Science Without Numbers* (1980) to performing this task on a portion of Newtonian mechanics.[12] Whether it can be completed for all of our best scientific theories (in particular, quantum mechanics and general relativity) is controversial. So even granting Musgrave some charity in his statement of the argument, the argument depends on the successful completion of Hartry Field's nominalisation of science.[13]

Before concluding this section I should address one other statement of the unfalsifiability worry that has been put forward. Charles Parsons writes, in response to the claim that mathematics is empirical:

> In one sense mathematics may change as a result [of theory change]: the theory of one type of structure may become more salient, that of another type less so. But no proposition of pure mathematics has been *falsified*. If we view mathematics in this light, no proposition of Euclidean geometry is falsified by the discovery that physical space is not Euclidean. (Parsons, 1983a, p. 196)

But, as Michael Resnik (1997) points out, the theory of Euclidean geometry *as a theory of physical space* was falsified. It remains unfalsified as an abstract theory of Euclidean spaces. This move to the abstract formulation, when a substantial mathematical theory of some physical structure is falsified, is what Resnik calls a *Euclidean Rescue*. The mathematical theory is seen as inappropriate to the given physical situation rather than as a falsified mathematical theory. Indeed, one could perform a similar manoeuvre on other parts of a theory when that theory is falsified. For example, one might think that the Ptolemy planetary model is unfalsified as an abstract theory (as opposed to a model of the solar system). But there seems little interest in such a rescue of Ptolemic astronomy.

The important difference, then, is not that mathematics is unfalsifiable; it's that we are inclined to perform Euclidean rescues only on mathematical theories. The reason for this, Quine points out, is that the vocabulary of mathematics (and logic) "pervades all branches of science, and consequently their truths and techniques are consequential in all branches of science" (1986, p. 399). He continues:

---

[12] In relation to this very point Field says: "It is *only relative to the assumption that we could carry out the program of showing mathematical entities to be eliminable* that the existence or non-existence of mathematical objects can be said to be beyond the range of possible evidence" (Field, 1993, p. 296) (Field's italics).

[13] I discussed this matter in chapter 4.

> This ... is why we are disinclined to tamper with logic or mathe-
> matics when a failure of prediction shows there is something wrong
> with our system of the world. We prefer to seek an adequate re-
> vision of some more secluded corner of science, where the change
> would not reverberate so widely through the system. (Quine, 1986,
> pp. 399–400)

So, to reiterate, it's not that mathematical theories are unfalsifiable in any
absolute sense; it's just that whenever they are part of a falsified pack-
age, the mathematical portion is usually salvaged for reasons of minimum
mutilation to the web of belief.

6.3   The Sober Objection

Elliott Sober's (1993) objection to the indispensability argument is framed
from the viewpoint of *contrastive empiricism*, so it will be necessary to first
consider some of the details of this theory in order to evaluate the force of
Sober's objection. As will become apparent, though, contrastive empiricism
has some difficulties that I'm inclined to think cannot be overcome. This
robs Sober's objection of much—but not all—of its force. In the final part
of this section, then, I will recast the objection without the contrastive
empiricism framework and show that this version of the objection also faces
significant difficulties.

6.3.1   Contrastive Empiricism

Contrastive empiricism is best understood as a position between scientific
realism and Bas van Fraassen's (1980) constructive empiricism. The central
idea of contrastive empiricism is the appeal to the *Likelihood Principle* as
a means of choosing between theories.

Principle 3 (The Likelihood Principle) *Observation O   favours hy-
pothesis H_1 over hypothesis H_2 iff $P(O|H_1) > P(O|H_2)$.*

It's clear from principle 3 that the support an hypothesis receives is a
relative matter. As Sober puts it (emphasis in original):

> The Likelihood Principle entails that the degree of support a theory
> enjoys should be understood relatively, not absolutely. A theory
> competes with other theories; observations reduce our uncertainty
> about this competition by discriminating among alternatives. The
> evidence we have for the theories we accept is evidence that favours
> those theories *over others*. (Sober, 1993, p. 39)

According to Sober, though, evidence can never favour one theory over all possible competitors since "[o]ur evidence is far less powerful, the range of alternatives that we consider far more modest" (Sober, 1993, p. 39).

Another consequence of principle 3 is that some observational data may fail to discriminate between two theories. For instance, contrastive empiricism cannot discriminate between standard geological and evolutionary theory, and Gosse's theory that the earth was created about 4,000 years ago with all the fossil records and so on in place. Indeed, Sober's account cannot rule out any cleverly formulated sceptical hypothesis. Furthermore, Sober is reluctant to appeal to simplicity or parsimoniousness as non-observational signs of truth, and so such sceptical problems are taken to be scientifically insoluble. This is one important way in which contrastive empiricism departs from standard scientific realism (and, arguably, standard scientific methodology).

Although according to contrastive empiricism "science attempts to solve discrimination problems" (Sober, 1993, p. 39) and the burden of solving these problems is placed firmly on the observational data, there is no restriction to hypotheses about observables, as in van Fraassen's (1980) constructive empiricism (emphasis in original):

> Contrastive empiricism differs from constructive empiricism in that the former does not limit science to the task of assigning truth values to hypotheses that are strictly about observables. What the hypotheses are *about* is irrelevant; what matters is that the competing hypotheses make different claims about what we can observe. Put elliptically, the difference between the two empiricisms is that constructive empiricism focuses on *propositions*, whereas contrastive empiricism focuses on *problems*. The former position says that science can assign truth values only to *propositions* of a particular sort; the latter says that science can solve *problems* only when they have a particular character. (Sober, 1993, p. 41)

Much more could be said about contrastive empiricism, but we have seen enough to motivate Sober's objection to indispensability theory.

6.3.2 The Objection

Sober's main objection is that if mathematics is confirmed along with our best empirical hypotheses, there must be mathematics-free competitors (or at least alternative mathematical theories as competitors):

> Formulating the indispensability argument in the format specified by the Likelihood Principle shows how unrealistic that argument is. For

example, do we really have alternative hypotheses to the hypotheses of arithmetic? If we could make sense of such alternatives, could they be said to confer probabilities on observations that differ from the probabilities entailed by the propositions of arithmetic themselves? I suggest that both these questions deserve negative answers. (Sober, 1993, pp. 45–46)

It is important to be clear about what Sober is claiming. He is *not* claiming that indispensability arguments are fatally flawed. He is not unfriendly to the general idea of ontological commitment to the indispensable entities of our best scientific theories. He simply denies that "a mathematical statement inherits the observational support that accrues to the empirically successful scientific theories in which it occurs" (Sober, 1993, p. 53). This is enough, though, to place him at odds with the Quine/Putnam version of the indispensability argument that I'm defending.

In reply to this objection, then, I wish to point out first that there *are* alternatives to number theory. Frege showed us how to express most numerical statements required by empirical science without recourse to quantifying over numbers.[14] Furthermore, depending on how much analysis you think Hartry Field has successfully nominalised, there are alternatives to that also. (At the very least he has suggested that there are nominalist alternatives to differential calculus.)[15]

I take the crux of Sober's objection then to be the second of his two questions, and I agree with him here that the answer to this question deserves a negative answer. I don't think that Field's version of Newtonian mechanics and standard Newtonian mechanics would confer different probabilities on any observational data, but so much the worse for contrastive empiricism. The question of which is the better theory will be decided on the grounds of simplicity, elegance, and so on—grounds explicitly ruled out by contrastive empiricism. Indispensability theory does not propose to settle all discrimination problems by purely empirical means, so of course it flounders when forced into the straight-jacket of contrastive empiricism.

You might be inclined to think that since a mathematised theory such as Newtonian mechanics and Field's nominalist counterpart have the same empirical consequences, it can't be said that the mathematics receives empirical support. According to this view, the mathematised version is preferred on the a priori grounds of simplicity, elegance and so on, *not* on

---

[14] For example, "There are two Fs" or "the number of the Fs is two" is written as:
$$(\exists x)(\exists y)(((Fx \& Fy) \& x \neq y) \& (\forall z)(Fz \supset (z = x \lor z = y))).$$

[15] This is only considering "sensible" alternatives. There are, presumably, many rather bad theories that do without mathematics. Perhaps most pseudosciences such as astrology and palm reading do without all but the most rudimentary mathematics.

empirical grounds. In reply to this, I simply point out that there is nothing special about the mathematical content of theories in this respect. As I've already mentioned, the reason we prefer standard evolutionary theory and geology over Gosse's version of creationism is for the same apparently a priori reasons. It would be a very odd view, however, that denied evolutionary theory and geology received empirical support. Surely the right thing to say here is that evolutionary theory and geology receive both empirical support *and* support from a priori considerations. I'm inclined to say the same for the mathematical cases.[16]

Another objection to the whole contrastive empiricism approach to theory choice is raised by Geoffrey Hellman and considered by Sober (1993). The objection is that often a theory is preferred over alternatives, not because it makes certain (correct) predictions that the other theories assign very low probabilities to, but rather, because it is the *only* theory to address such phenomena at all.[17] Sober points out that the relevance of this to the question of the indispensability of mathematics is that presumably "stronger mathematical assumptions facilitate empirical predictions that cannot be obtained from weaker mathematics" (Sober, 1993, p. 52).[18] If this objection stands, then the central thesis of contrastive empiricism is thrown into conflict with actual scientific practice. For a naturalist this almost amounts to a reductio of the position. Indeed, Sober admits that "[i]f this point were correct, it would provide a quite general refutation of contrastive empiricism" (Sober, 1993, p. 52). I believe that Hellman's point is correct, but first let's consider Sober's reply.

Sober's first point is that when scientists are faced with a theory with no relevant competitors, they can contrast the theory in question with its own negation. He considers the example of Newtonian physics correctly predicting the return of Halley's comet, something on which other theories were completely silent. Sober claims, however, that "alternatives to Newtonian theory can be constructed from Newtonian laws themselves" (1993, p. 52).

---

[16] It is perhaps best to speak of the "scientific justification of theories," where this includes empirical support *and* support from a priori considerations. This is clearly the sort of support that our best scientific theories receive, so we see that Sober's concentration on purely empirical support skews the whole debate. (Cf. section 4.3.) Thanks to Bernard Linsky for a useful discussion on this point.

[17] Hellman (1999) gives the example of relativistic physics correctly predicting the relationship between total energy and relativistic mass. In pre-relativistic physics no such relationship is even postulated, indeed, questions about such a relationship cannot even be posed.

[18] For example, Geoffrey Hellman (1992) argues that the weaker constructivist mathematics, such as that of the intuitionists (cf. Heyting (1931) and Dummett(1975)), will not allow the empirical predictions facilitated by the stronger methods of standard analysis.

For example, Newton's law of universal gravitation:[19]

$$F = \frac{Gm_1m_2}{r^2}$$

competes with:

$$F = \frac{Gm_1m_2}{r^3}$$

and

$$F = \frac{Gm_1m_2}{r^4}$$

and many others. There is no doubt that such alternatives *can be* constructed and contrasted with Newtonian theory, but surely we are not interested in what scientists *could do*; we are interested in *actual scientific practice*.

Sober takes this a little further though when he claims that this *is* standard scientific practice for such cases (1993, pp. 52–53). He offers no evidence in support of this last claim, and without a thorough investigation of the history of relevant episodes in the history of science it seems quite implausible. It seems extremely unlikely that scientists were interested in debating over whether it should be r^2, r^3, or r^4 in the law of universal gravitation, as Sober suggests.[20] The relevant debate would have surely been over retaining the existing theory or adopting Newtonian theory. At the very least, Sober needs to present some evidence to suggest that scientists are inclined to contrast a theory with its own negation when nothing better is on offer. Until such time, I'm inclined to think he is wrong about this.

In his second point in response to Hellman's objection, he considers the possibility of "strong" mathematics allowing empirical predictions that cannot be replicated using weaker mathematics. He points out that strong mathematics also allows the formulation of theories that make false predictions, and that this is ignored by the indispensability argument (emphasis in original):

> It is a striking fact that mathematics allows us to construct theories that make *true* predictions and that we could not construct such

---

[19] Here F is the gravitational force exerted on two particles of mass m_1 and m_2 separated by a distance r, and G is the gravitational constant.

[20] Not to mention $r^{2.0000000000001}$ or $r^{1.9999999999999}$. (Although it seems that cases such as these *were* considered when the problems with Mercury's perihelion came to light (Roseveare (1983)), they were considered only in order to save the essentials of Newtonian theory, which, by that stage, was already a highly confirmed theory.)

predictively *successful* theories without mathematics. It is less often noticed that mathematics allows us to construct theories that make *false* predictions and that we could not construct such predictively *unsuccessful* theories without mathematics. If the authority of mathematics depended on its empirical track record, *both* these patterns should matter to us. The fact that we do not doubt the mathematical parts of empirically *unsuccessful* theories is something we should not forget. Empirical testing does not allow one to ignore the bad news and listen only to the good. (Sober, 1993, p. 53)

The first question is: How is this supposed to disarm the Hellman objection? It may be useful at this point to spell out how I take the Hellman strategy to proceed. Hellman's point is that contrastive empiricism does not account for cases where a theory is preferred because it makes predictions that no other theory is able to address one way or another. If this is accepted, then contrastive empiricism as a representation of how theory choice is achieved seems at best only part of the story, and at worst completely misguided. Furthermore, if it is reasonable to prefer some theory because it correctly predicts new phenomena that other theories are silent on, then it is reasonable to accept strong mathematical hypotheses, since theories employing strong mathematics are able to predict just such phenomena.

I take it that Sober's reply runs like this: Contrastive empiricism can accommodate the Hellman examples of scientific theories that address new phenomena. This is done by contrasting such theories with their negations. Thus, a general undermining of contrastive empiricism is avoided. This reply, however, seems to allow that strong mathematics is confirmed, because such theories correctly predict empirical phenomena that theories employing weaker mathematics cannot address. So the cost of saving contrastive empiricism from the Hellman objection is that Sober's original point against the empirical confirmation of mathematics now fails. Here is where the second part of Sober's reply is called upon. The point here is simply that the case of strong mathematics is different from that of bold new physical theories in that strong mathematics can also facilitate false predictions that competing theories are silent on. Thus, the mathematics cannot share the credit for the successful empirical predictions, since it won't share the blame for unsuccessful empirical predictions. (One admires Sober's sense of justice here, but as we shall see, it is misplaced.)

There are a couple of interesting issues raised by this rejoinder. First, the rejoinder is in the context of a defence of contrastive empiricism and yet it is not an argument for that thesis. Neither is it an argument depending on contrastive empiricism. It seems like a new objection to the use of indispensability arguments to gain conclusions about mathematical entities.

What is more, this objection appears to be independent of his contrastive empiricism and as such is the more substantial part of his objection to indispensability theory.

6.3.3   A Residual Worry

So far I've pointed out that I think Sober is quite wrong about scientists contrasting bold new theories with their negations. At the very least he needs to give some evidence to support his claim that they do.[21] Indeed, it would be interesting to investigate some candidate cases in detail to shed some light on this issue, but fortunately this is not necessary for our purposes, since even if I grant Sober his first point (that contrastive empiricism can accommodate Hellman's examples of bold new theories), the second part of his reply also runs into trouble.

Sober claims, in effect, that mathematical theories cannot enjoy the confirmation received by theories that make bold new true predictions because the mathematics is not disconfirmed when it is employed by a theory that makes bold new false predictions. I've already noted that this point is stated independently of contrastive empiricism. Indeed, I take this to be a separate worry about the indispensability argument as applied to mathematical entities. Also bear in mind that it is important to his case that there be a difference between mathematical hypotheses and non-mathematical hypotheses in this respect.

This last claim, though, is false. Many non-mathematical hypotheses can be employed by false theories and not be held responsible for the disconfirmation. Hypotheses about electrons (notoriously) have been employed by many false theories, and yet we are unwilling to blame them for the lack of empirical support for the theories in question. Astrologers refer to the orbits of the planets in grossly false theories about human behaviour, and yet we are not about to blame the planets for the lack of empirical support for astrology. It is surely one of the important tasks of scientists to decide which parts of a falsified theory are in need of revision and which are not. Sober would have us throw out the baby with the bathwater, it seems.

Hellman (1999) points out that this partial asymmetry between confirmation and disconfirmation is a consequence of confirmational holism. When a theory is confirmed, the *whole* theory is confirmed. When it is disconfirmed, it is rarely the fault of every part of the theory, and so the guilty part is to be found and dispensed with. It's analogous to a sensitive

---

[21] It is worth pointing out that he must provide evidence that contrasting theories with their negations is a general phenomenon. Even if there are only one or two counterexamples, contrastive empiricism is in trouble.

computer program. If the program delivers the correct results, then every part of the program is believed to be correct. However, if it is not working, it is often because of only one small error. The job of the computer programmer (in part) is to seek out the faulty part of the program and correct it. Furthermore, the programmer will resort to wholesale changes to the program only if no other solution presents itself. This is especially evident when one part of the program *is* working. In such a case the programmer seeks to make a small *local* change in the defective part of the program. Changing the programming language, for instance, is *not* such a change.

Now if we return to Sober's charge that mathematics cannot enjoy the credit for confirmation of a theory if it cannot share the blame for disconfirmation, we see that blaming mathematics for the failure of some theory is never going to be a small local change, due to the simple fact that mathematics is used almost everywhere in science. What is more, much of that science is working perfectly well! Blaming the mathematics is like a programmer blaming the computer language. And similarly claiming that mathematics cannot share the credit is like claiming that the computer language cannot share the credit for the successful program. In some cases it may well be the fault of the mathematics or the language, but it is not a good strategy to start with changes to these.

Furthermore, we see that mathematics is not alone in this respect. Many clearly empirical hypotheses share this feature of apparent immunity from blame for disconfirmation. Michael Resnik points out that conservation principles seem immune from liability for much the same reasons as mathematics. He goes even further to express doubts about whether such principles could be tested at all in the contrastive empiricist framework and "yet we do not want to be forced to deny them empirical content or to hold that the general theories containing them have not been tested experimentally" (Resnik, 1995, p. 168). Another such empirical hypothesis is the hypothesis that space-time is continuous rather than discrete and dense.

To sum up, then. I agree with Sober that there is a problem of reconciling contrastive empiricism with indispensability theory, but for the most part this is because of general problems with the former. In particular, contrastive empiricism fails to give an adequate account of a theory being adopted because it correctly predicts phenomena that its competitors are unable to speak to at all. I agree with Hellman here that this looks like the kind of role mathematics plays in theory selection. Strong mathematics allows the formulation of theories that address phenomena on which other theories are completely silent. Sober's rejoinder is that mathematical hypotheses are different from other scientific hypotheses, in that mathematical hypotheses allow false predictions just as readily as true ones, and yet mathematics remains blameless for the former. This rejoinder is in effect a new argument against indispensability theory applied to mathematical entities and, what is more, it is independent of the framework of contrastive empiricism. Nevertheless, the rejoinder faces problems of its own. First, it seems to misrepresent the type of holism at issue—the holism at issue has an asymmetry between confirmation and disconfirmation built into it. Second, it seems clear that mathematics is not alone in its apparent immunity from blame in cases of disconfirmation.

Before closing I should mention Sober's claim that the main point of his objection can be separated to some extent from the contrastive empiricist epistemology. He does not, however, seem to have the residual worry that I discussed in mind. He is concerned that you might think that contrastive empiricism can't be right because it ignores nonempirical criteria such as simplicity. He then suggests that "even proponents of such nonempirical criteria should be able to agree that *empirical* considerations must be mediated by likelihoods" (Sober, 1993, p. 55). Sober is suggesting that at the very least we discriminate between empirical hypotheses by appeal to likelihoods and that his objection goes through granting only this.[22] But why should we accept that all discriminations between empirical hypotheses must be mediated by likelihoods? After all, we have already seen that we cannot discriminate between the hypothesis that space-time is continuous and the hypothesis that space-time is discrete and dense on empirical grounds and yet these are surely both empirical hypotheses. So Sober's objections to indispensability theory fail because they depend crucially on accepting the Likelihood Principle as the only arbiter on empirical matters. The independent residual worry that I identified in section 3 fails because it doesn't take account of the asymmetric character of confirmational holism.

6.4   Is Mathematics Contingent?

So far I have argued that according to indispensability theory mathematical knowledge is a posteriori. Does this imply that mathematical entities are contingent? That is, does the indispensability argument give us reason to believe that there are mathematical entities, but that there might not have been? Although I'm inclined to think that mathematics *is* contingent, it may be that indispensabilists can go either way on this issue.[23] After all,

---

[22] Since, according to indispensability theory, mathematics *is* empirical, and yet we cannot discriminate between mathematical and non-mathematical theories by appeal to likelihoods.

[23] Quine, in fact, does not even want to use modal talk unless such talk is understood as context and interest relative. It's fair to say, however, that he believes in mathematical entities whose existence is not necessary.

Kripke (1980) has shown us how we can have a posteriori necessary truth.[24] I won't pursue this line of thought though. I just wish to point out that there is an alternative to the view that mathematical objects are contingent and that this alternative is, at least at face value, consistent with the view that mathematical knowledge is a posteriori. Instead, I want to consider what is perhaps a more natural position for an indispensabilist to adopt— that mathematical entities exist contingently—and to defend this position against some recent objections from Bob Hale and Crispin Wright.

Hale and Wright (1992; 1994) have criticised Hartry Field for his belief in the contingent non-existence of mathematical entities. According to Field, there are no mathematical objects, but there might have been. Hale and Wright, on the other hand, believe that mathematical entities exist *necessarily*. Thus, Hale and Wright take issue with Field on both the non-existence claim and the contingency claim, but here I'll focus on the debate over the latter. Before discussing their objections it will be helpful, I think, to consider briefly why it is that Field is committed to the contingent non-existence of mathematical entities.

As was discussed in chapter 4, Field relies on the concept of conservativeness in his fictional account of mathematics and this concept is explained in terms of, and indeed entails, consistency. This latter concept, Hale and Wright point out (1992, p. 112), is something that nominalists need to be very careful about, since both the usual syntactic and semantic accounts quantify over abstracta—sequences of sentences in the former and models in the latter. Field of course is aware of this and so explains consistency in primitively modal terms. Furthermore, on Field's account, the meaning of the "it is consistent that" operator is not conveyed by definition but by rules of use (Field, 1993, p. 290). The upshot of all this is that according to Field, a consistent theory is one that is possibly true (in Field's primitive sense of possibility, of course). This means that if the Peano axioms are consistent, then they are possibly true. Thus, since Field believes that they are in fact false, they must be contingently false (again assuming their consistency).

Field, it seems, has no choice but to accept contingent nominalism.[25] As I've already mentioned, I think that contingent Platonism[26] is a rather natural position for the mathematical realist motivated by indispensability

---

[24] Kripke takes identity statements, if true, to be necessarily true. However, the truth of such identity statements cannot be found by purely a priori means. Examples include Phosphorus is Hesperus and water is H_2O.

[25] This is the view that it is contingent whether mathematical entities exist or not, and in fact they do not.

[26] This is the view that it is contingent whether mathematical entities exist or not, and in fact they do.

considerations to adopt, but that this position is not compulsory. Still I'm inclined to think that contingent Platonism is correct and so I find myself on Field's side in this debate, since, as Field points out, although the Hale and Wright attack is directed mostly against contingent nominalism, "it is clear that if their arguments ... were correct, they would also undermine 'contingent platonism'" (Field, 1993, p. 285). So let me discuss what I take to be Hale and Wright's two main arguments against the contingency of mathematical entities. Although the first objection does not succeed (and this seems to be conceded by Hale and Wright (1994, p. 175), it is worth considering this objection because the underlying intuition is clearer in this objection than in the second.

6.4.1   What Is the Contingency Contingent On?

Hale and Wright's first objection to the contingency of the existence or non-existence of mathematical objects is that such a contingency would need to be contingent on something (emphasis in original):

> It is deeply rooted in our ordinary conception of contingency that there ought in general to be explanations of *why* things which might have been the case are not the case, and of *why* things are the case which might not have been the case. But in the present kind of instance—the existence of the integers, or real numbers, for example—there is not even a glimmering of how such an explanation might proceed. This seems a strong sign that the notion of contingency would be *misapplied* in the present context, and hence that there is philosophical error in any assumptions that commit Field to so applying it. (Hale and Wright, 1992, p. 115)

Field's reply to this is to point out that the conception of possibility at issue (for the explanation of consistency) is *logical* possibility not *conceptual* possibility[27] and that it is a mistake to expect an account of what every *logical* contingency is contingent on (Field, 1989, p. 43). As Field points out,

> there are surely senses of "contingent" in which saying that God's non-existence is contingent would leave us wanting an account of what it is contingent on; for instance, if by calling it contingent we meant that some alternative historical developments might have

---

[27] A statement is logically possible (for Field) just in case it is not first-order logically contradictory. A statement is conceptually possible (roughly) just in case its negation is not true by virtue of its meaning (Field, 1993, p. 292).

brought God into existence. But surely granting the consistency of the existence of God (together with the actuality or at least consistency of God's non-existence) is not granting the contingency of God's non-existence in *that* sense of contingency. I fail to see how the case of numbers is relevantly different. (Field, 1993, pp. 291–292)

Nonetheless, Field grants that the existence of mathematical entities is also *conceptually* contingent (1993, p. 285) (he just denies that this follows from consideration of conservativeness), and this also seems the most plausible reading of "contingency" for the mathematical realist persuaded by indispensability theory.

Now to Hale and Wright's claim that all conceptual contingencies require explanation for their obtaining or not obtaining. Field points out that this claim admits clear counterexamples, besides the mathematical case:

On the question of why there are no numbers, my view is that this is like why is there matter, or why are there no immaterial minds, or why is there no God: you simply can't expect there to be an answer to such basic existence and non-existence questions ('basic' in the sense of: applied to a whole 'ontological category'). (Private correspondence from Field quoted in Hale and Wright (1992, p. 127))

Field is surely correct here. Hale and Wright are also quick to admit this and even provide other examples of contingencies that do not seem to admit explanation, such as: Why is there something rather than nothing? Such examples lead Hale and Wright (1994, p. 174) to refine their principle that *all* contingencies require explanation and offer the following in its place:

Principle 4 *It is contingent that p only if* either *there could be an explanation why p or there is available a priori an explanation why the (putative) fact that p must resist explanation.*

The first and most obvious problem is that this principle is extremely ad hoc. The move to requiring a *possible* explanation rather than an *actual* explanation is completely unmotivated.

I agree, however, that *something* ought to be said about when an explanation for conceptual contingencies should be forthcoming. On the model of explanation offered by Philip Kitcher (1981) (which both Field and I are partial to) something can be said about such matters, but in many cases it will not be obvious whether to expect an explanation for certain phenomena in advance. This is because, on Kitcher's account, explanation consists in reducing the number of independent phenomena. That is, explanation may be seen as unification. So this account "does not give explainability the kind of default status that Hale and Wright assume" (Field, 1993, p. 295). Explanation is desirable but not to be expected—indeed one expects that some phenomena must resist explanation.

Although I believe that the ad hoc nature of principle 4 is sufficient for its rejection, and consequently the rejection of the objection that rests on it, there are other problems with this objection. Field points out (1993, pp. 294–295) that Hale and Wright's refined principles (such as principle 4) fare little better against some of the non-mathematical counterexamples, such as any truth of the form "it is a fundamental law of physics that *P*." Indeed, Hale and Wright concede as much (1994, p. 175) and decline to press this objection any further but instead pursue a related argument: the argument from insularity.

6.4.2   The Argument from Insularity

Let us call some proposition *brute* if whether or not it obtains does not depend on anything else. Call a proposition *barren* if no phenomena depend on whether it obtains or not. Call a proposition *absolutely insular* if it is both brute and barren. Also note that if Field's program of showing mathematics to be dispensable to science can be carried out, then claims about mathematical entities would appear to be absolutely insular. Absolute insularity, though, is metaphysically dubious. This is something that all the participants in this debate agree. The question is what is the correct anti-insularity principle. Hale and Wright (1992, pp. 133–134) suggest the following:

Principle 5 (Hale and Wright's Anti-insularity Principle) *There are no absolutely insular conceptual contingencies.*

If Field's program is successful, claims about mathematical entities would be absolutely insular and so by principle 5 it could not be conceptually contingent whether mathematical entities exist or not.

Field, however, thinks that principle 5 is the wrong anti-insularity principle and I agree with him on this. To see this, he suggests the following example:

> Call something a *surdon* iff
>
> (A) its existence and state are in no way dependent on the existence and state of anything else; and
>
> (B) the existence and state of nothing else are in any way dependent on the existence and state of it.
>
> This certainly seems to be a conceptually consistent concept; but (A) and (B) guarantee insularity, so principle [5] immediately guarantees

the existence of surdons—indeed, the conceptual necessity of their existence. Of course, Hale and Wright accept this conclusion, since they take numbers to be surdons, but even they should balk at the idea that establishing the existence of mathematical entities is as easy as this! (Field, 1993, pp. 296–297)

Field concludes that principle 5 can't be right. The correct anti-insularity principle he suggests is:

Principle 6 (Field's Anti-insularity Principle) *We should not (at least without very compelling reason) assume the existence of absolutely insular entities.*

Thus, according to Field, "unless mathematical entities prove indispensable, we ought not to believe in them" (Field, 1993, p. 297).

To this, Hale and Wright reply that Field has misconstrued their original argument:

> Our objection was not that Field's view of the (putative) fact that there are no numbers infringes an evidently acceptable principle [principle 5], but that it forces an unmotivated decision against an attractive principle. (Hale and Wright, 1994, p. 180)

But surely Field's belief in the contingent existence of mathematical entities is not *unmotivated*. He has very good theoretical grounds for doing so and he makes this clear in a number of places. Furthermore, he does not rule principle 5 out of play without offering a suitable replacement (principle 6). What is more, his example of surdons demonstrates a point in favour of his own principle 6 over Hale and Wright's principle 5.[28]

Where does this leave us then? Hale and Wright claim that contingent nominalism would violate principle 5 and since the latter is an attractive metaphysical principle it ought not be forced out of play without good reason. Note that this same objection won't work against the contingent Platonism offered by the indispensability argument, since the reason for believing that there are mathematical entities is precisely because such entities are not absolutely insular. Thus, on this account, the contingent existence of mathematical entities would not violate Hale and Wright's principle 5.

---

[28] Hale and Wright (1994, pp. 181–183) disagree that on their account Platonism is obtained as easily as Field suggests in the above quotation. They claim that conceptual consistency only defeasibly justifies claims of possibility. Thus, the conceptual consistency of surdons does not guarantee their necessary existence. Even granting Hale and Wright this, it seems that principle 6 is at least as plausible as principle 5, and so Field is not guilty of an unmotivated rejection of "an attractive principle."

There is something odd about this though. Hale and Wright make it quite clear that it is *contingency* that is unpalatable.[29] Why should they be any less concerned by contingent Platonism than contingent nominalism? This is another reason to suggest that principle 5 is not the correct anti-insularity principle.[30] In any case, their final argument against Field, even if it were correct, does not seem to undermine contingent Platonism. I'm inclined to agree with Field, though, that there is nothing problematic about either contingent nominalism or contingent Platonism.

[29] Wright, in an earlier formulation of the concern, states this quite explicitly (emphasis in original):

> Field has no prospect of an account of what the alleged contingency is contingent *on*. The world does not, in Field's view, but might have contained numbers. But there is no explanation of *why* it contains no numbers; and if it had contained numbers, there would have been no explanation of that either. There are no conditions favourable for the emergence of numbers, and no conditions which prevent their emergence. (Wright, 1988, p. 465)

[30] See Colyvan (2000) for more on this debate.

7

Conclusion

So far I've outlined the Quinean indispensability argument and demonstrated its reliance on the doctrines of holism and naturalism (chapter 1). I then discussed these doctrines, taking particular care to spell out exactly how each is to be understood, since there is more than one variety of each of these in the literature (chapter 2). In the process of examining naturalism we saw that the Quinean reading of this important doctrine is crucial to the indispensability argument, so in chapter 3 I defended the Quinean variety of naturalism against its main competitor. Chapters 4 through 6 were devoted to defending the indispensability argument against some of its critics. Most notable of these are: Field, who denies that mathematics is indispensable to science (chapter 4); Maddy, who questions whether confirmational holism is consistent with Quinean naturalism (chapter 5); and Sober, who questions whether the mathematical content of scientific theories accrues empirical support in the way Quine suggests (section 6.3). If you're convinced by my discussion so far, then you have good cause to accept mathematical entities into your ontology. But you're entitled to ask a little more about the nature of the mathematical entities you're accepting.

We've already seen (from chapter 6) that one consequence of the indispensability argument is that mathematical knowledge has an empirical character. This means that our knowledge of mathematical entities is a posteriori. I've also suggested that it is plausible that mathematical knowledge is contingent. There are other questions to be answered though: Does the indispensability argument yield acausal mathematical entities or does it tell us that mathematical entities are causally active after all? Does it tell us that we ought to believe in sets and sets alone, because we can "build" the rest of the mathematical universe out of them? Does it tell us

141

whether sets are sui generis or universals (or something else)? Until now I've been completely silent on all such questions, and for good reason—the indispensability argument, as I've presented it, is completely silent on all these issues. I'll elaborate on this claim in the next section.

7.1   What the Argument Doesn't Show

Although Quine has definite and well-developed views on many of the issues I raised, it is important to distinguish which of these views depend on the indispensability argument and which depend on other philosophical doctrines. For example, Quine believes that all mathematical entities are sets of some sort or another. Why does he believe this? There's nothing in the indispensability argument that forces this conclusion. Rather, it is a consequence of his extreme Ockhamist tendencies. As Paul Benacerraf puts it (on behalf of Quine), "why demand more than sets, if sets is all you need?" (Benacerraf, 1996, p. 28). There's nothing in the indispensability argument that prevents someone with less stark tastes from accepting the whole gamut of mathematical entities. But, the Ockhamist might cry, that's to ignore the well-known reductions of numbers to sets, ordered pairs to sets, functions to ordered pairs, and so on. Without the Ockhamist's taste for desert landscapes,[1] however, it's not clear what these reductions show. It is an interesting fact about mathematics that the natural numbers, for instance, can be modelled in set theory, but this on its own does not tell us that sets and not numbers exist.[2]

As for the question of whether sets (and other mathematical objects) are sui generis or not, again the indispensability argument says nothing. It simply asserts that there *are* mathematical objects. They might be constituted by more mundane items such as universals and/or relations (as John Bigelow (1988), Peter Forrest and David Armstrong (1987) claim), patterns or structures (as Michael Resnik (1997) and Stewart Shapiro (1997) claim) or the part/whole relation (as David Lewis (1991) claims). Perhaps they are constituted by *more* exotic items such as possible structures (as Hilary Putnam (1967) and Geoffrey Hellman (1989) claim). In short, any (realist) account of mathematical objects is all right by the indispensability argument. It must, of course, be consistent with the view that mathematics has an empirical character (which is the only real restriction). It is reasonable to assume, however, that the latter can be tacked onto most views easily enough (with the exception of explicitly non-empirical accounts such

---

[1] This phrase, of course, is due to Quine, who says that an "overpopulated universe ... offends the aesthetic sense of us who have a taste for desert landscapes" (1948, p. 4).

[2] Paul Benacerraf (1965, pp. 289–290) also makes this point.

as Crispin Wright's (1983)).

The question of whether the indispensability argument delivers causal or acausal mathematical entities is a little more complicated. At least some people believe that it delivers causally active entities. Since I think that this is a mistake, I'll discuss the issue in some detail, using an article by Colin Cheyne and Charles Pigden (1996) as my foil. I'll argue that Cheyne and Pigden are mistaken and that the issue of the causal nature of mathematical entities is left open by indispensability theory.

Cheyne and Pigden present their case as a challenge to mathematical Platonism.[3] The challenge is directed at those Platonists who rely on the Quine/Putnam indispensability argument. As we already know, such Platonists believe the indispensability of mathematics to our best scientific theories gives us good reason to suppose that mathematical entities exist. The Cheyne/Pigden challenge is simply to give an account of how causally inert mathematical entities could be indispensable to science. Failing to meet this challenge, Cheyne and Pigden claim, would place Platonism in a no-win situation: Either Hartry Field's nominalisation of science is successful, in which case mathematical entities are dispensable to science, or Field's program fails, in which case mathematical entities may indeed be taken to be indispensable to science, but the best explanation for their indispensability is that they are not causally inert as the Platonist assumes. Either way Platonism loses. I will argue that Platonism is well equipped to meet this challenge—it is not the bad bet Cheyne and Pigden suggest.

Since there is little disagreement that the indispensability argument is without any force if Field's program of nominalising science is successful, we need only consider what follows from the failure of Field's program. Let's suppose, then, that Field's program fails and that this gives us good reason to believe mathematical entities to be indispensable to our best scientific theories. Cheyne and Pigden are unsatisfied with what you might think of as "brute fact" indispensability—the view that we ought to believe in any entity that is indispensable to science and there is no more to be said about it. They would like some account of why it is that mathematical entities are indispensable to science.[4] This much of their challenge seems quite reasonable, but they wish to push the point further:

Why should theories which quantify over certain objects do better

---

[3] In fact their challenge is directed at what they call "standard Platonism." This is the view that mathematical objects have mind independent existence and that such objects have neither causal powers nor spatio-temporal location. It is to be contrasted with other versions of mathematical realism in which mathematical entities *are* located in space-time *and/or* have causal powers.

[4] See also Balaguer (1996b) and Kitcher (1984, pp. 104–105) for similar worries.

than theories which do not? One explanation is ready to hand. If we are genuinely unable to leave those objects out of our best theory of what the world is like ... , then they must be responsible in some way for the world's being the way it is. In other words, their indispensability is explained by the fact that they are causally affecting the world, however indirectly. The indispensability argument may yet be compelling, but it would seem to be a compelling argument for the existence of entities *with* causal powers. (Cheyne and Pigden, 1996, p. 641)

It is also clear that Cheyne and Pigden think this is not just "one explanation ready to hand" but the *only* plausible explanation.

This passage is puzzling for two reasons. First, the indispensability of a certain entity to some theory says no more than that the entity plays an important (explanatory) role in the theory in question. If you also believe that all explanation is causal explanation (or at least all explanation *of events* is causal explanation), then it looks as though the entity in question is indeed causally active, but why believe it otherwise? At the very least it seems Cheyne and Pigden have left out a crucial (and controversial) premise from their argument from indispensability to causal activity.[5] If they do not believe that all explanation is causal, then their argument has little force. Furthermore, even if mathematical entities *are* taken to be causally active, Cheyne and Pigden give little indication of how this explains their indispensability. Presumably not all causally active entities are indispensable to science,[6] so if some entity's indispensability to a theory is to be explained, more needs to be said than "the entity in question is causally active." In short, Cheyne and Pigden's explanation for the indispensability of mathematical entities is not satisfying as it stands. This takes much of the pressure off the Platonist to provide a better explanation.[7]

The second difficulty with Cheyne and Pigden's argument comes from their failure to say anything about what they take causation to be. This might seem a harsh criticism since a discussion of causation is a large task that is somewhat tangential to their article. This may be, but their tentative conclusion that the indispensability argument is an argument for

---

[5] I discussed and dismissed the view that all explanation is causal in section 3.3.

[6] For example, consider two causally active entities, a and b say, both able to cause some event e, although, as a matter of fact, only one entity (suppose it's a) causes e. Now if we have a theory that already makes extensive appeal to b but doesn't seriously entertain the possibility of a existing at all, then it seems reasonable to believe that b is the cause of e and so a is completely dispensable despite its causal activity.

[7] It may well be that the general problem of explaining the indispensability of theoretical entities is a difficult task and the problem of explaining the indispensability of mathematical entities is just a special case of this problem.

causally active mathematical entities seems to revolve around a fairly undis-criminating notion of causation. On a more discriminating notion these same mathematical entities may be causally inert as the (standard) Pla-tonist claims. It looks as though Cheyne and Pigden get their conclusion by taking a rather idiosyncratic notion of causation. Allow me to elaborate.

The point Cheyne and Pigden are making is that the world would be different if there were no mathematical entities; therefore, mathematical entities are, in some sense at least, partially a cause of the way the world is. This is clearly some form of counterfactual theory of causation and in a later passage, when discussing how Sherlock Holmes might deduce that Moriarty is the murderer by the fact that there are three cigarettes in the ashtray, they give another clue as to what this notion of causation is:

> If the number two or the number four were in [three's] place, the effects would differ. What more is needed for it to qualify as an object with causal powers? (Cheyne and Pigden, 1996, p. 642)

I take it that the "effects" referred to in this passage are not necessarily the effects of the presence of the number three; otherwise, it appears that the argument is circular, since whether the number three has causal power is precisely what is at issue here. Instead, I take it that they mean (something like) the future light cones of the world would be different had a different number of cigarettes been present in the ashtray. Does it now follow that the number three is an object with causal powers? If not, then their argu-ment simply doesn't work, but if it does then we see how undiscriminating their notion of causation is. It implies, for instance, that the angle sum of a triangle *causes* bodies to be accelerated, since if the angle sum of a triangle is π radians, the space is (locally) Euclidean and so massive bodies experience no net force; if the angle sum is not π radians, the space would be non-Euclidean and hence any massive body would be experiencing a net force. Thus, if there were a change in the angle sum of a triangle, the future light cone of the world would be different in that it would contain an accelerated body.

If Cheyne and Pigden take causation to be simple counterfactual de-pendence, as it seems they do, their conclusion that the indispensability argument gives us good reason to believe in causally active mathematical entities isn't nearly as startling as it first seems. Mathematical entities might be causally active, but we're not talking about any common sense of "causally active" here. (After all, we're *not* inclined to think that an-gle sums of triangles can cause bodies to be accelerated.) Furthermore, such a simple counterfactual-dependence theory of causation doesn't agree with current theories of causation where, for instance, exchanges of energy and/or momentum are involved in causal processes.[8] Perhaps their conclusion that mathematical entities are causally active could be less misleadingly stated as "mathematical entities make a difference." Platonists would have no quarrel with this.

Although the argument from indispensability to causal activity doesn't succeed, there is still something to the original Cheyne/Pigden challenge. How could causally inert entities play an indispensable role in our best scientific theories? This question is answered by looking at the role such entities play in the relevant theories. The case here is no different from that of other theoretical entities. We don't conclude that electrons are causally active simply *because* they play an indispensable role in our theories of fundamental particles; we conclude that they are causally active because *of the role* they play in those theories. So too with mathematical entities. We must look at the role they play in our scientific theories. This role is, at least prima facie, not causal. What role do they play then? One possibility considered by Cheyne and Pigden is that "they provide a sort of metaphysical framework" for physics (1996, p. 643). I agree with Cheyne and Pigden that much work needs to be done on this "framework" theory if it is to be anything more than a metaphor. This, however, is not why Cheyne and Pigden reject the view.

They reject the view that mathematical entities are required as a framework to our best scientific theories because they mistakenly believe that it would have to be a framework "for any possible physics" (1996, p. 643). They believe that Hartry Field's (partial) nominalisation of Newtonian physics shows that mathematical entities are not indispensable to *all* possible physics:

> The new problem that the platonists face is this: how can a set of necessary beings help explain a contingent set of facts (namely, the facts accounted for by Einsteinian physics), when they would not be needed if the facts were otherwise (i.e., such as to confirm Newtonian physics)? (Cheyne and Pigden, 1996, p. 643)

Now their point may present problems for a Platonist who holds the "necessary framework" view, but it completely misses the target of the indispensabilist who denies that mathematical entities are necessary. I've already suggested that the latter is a very plausible position for an indispensabilist to adopt, and indeed it's the position that I adopt. I do *not* claim that mathematical entities are necessary entities or even necessary for any possible physics. I might well concede that were we to live in a

---

[8] For example, see Ellis (1990).

Newtonian world, we would have no reason to believe in mathematical entities,[9] but we don't live in such a world! In this, the actual, world we need mathematical entities to do our physics (or so we are assuming for the purposes of this discussion), and so we cannot dismiss the role mathematical entities play in the actual world because they play no such role in another possible world. I've already suggested (in section 6.4) that the most plausible view for the Quinean indispensabilist is that mathematical entities are believed to exist *contingently* and that this is because of the role they play in *this* world.

It seems that Cheyne and Pigden's claim, that the best explanation for the indispensability of mathematical entities to science is that those entities do, in fact, have causal powers, is unsupported unless they make the further claim that all explanation is causal, and I've already argued (section 3.3) that this is not so. In any case, given the simple counterfactual model of causation they seem to endorse, it looks as though causally active mathematical entities are the least of the unintuitive consequences. I also reject their assessment of the prospects of Platonists meeting their challenge by way of the "framework" role of mathematics. On the contrary, I think once Cheyne and Pigden's confusion over the modal status of the framework is cleared away, we see that the view that mathematical entities are contingent has the makings of a very good reply to their challenge. I conclude that the question of the causal capabilities of mathematical entities is left open by the indispensability argument.

7.2   The Benacerraf Challenges

I noted at the beginning of chapter 1 that mathematical ontology is discussed in the light of three arguments. So far I have been advocating belief in Platonism based on detailed consideration of one of these arguments—the indispensability argument. I'll now take a rather cursory look at the other two arguments—Benacerraf's problems for Platonism—and consider what resources a Quinean indispensabilist has on hand to deal with them. Obviously the details of the replies will depend on the exact details of the account of mathematics, and, as I've been at pains to point out, the indispensability argument leaves this issue relatively open. Nevertheless, I can at least make a few remarks toward disarming Benacerraf's concerns.

---

[9] Assuming, of course, that Newtonian physics is suitably nominalised.

7.2.1   What Numbers Could Not Be

In his famous essay "What Numbers Could Not Be" (1965), Benacerraf set
out to undermine the prevailing view that numbers could be reduced to
sets. This he did by pointing out that there is no unique reduction of the
natural numbers to sets. For instance, we could have $3 = \{\emptyset, \{\emptyset\}, \{\emptyset, \{\emptyset\}\}\}$
(Zermelo's three) or $3 = \{\{\{\emptyset\}\}\}$ (von Neumann's three). Benacerraf then
considers possible reasons for preferring one reduction over others, before
deciding that there are no such reasons:

> [I]f the number 3 is really one set rather than another, it must be
> possible to give some cogent reason for thinking so; for the position
> that this is an unknowable truth is hardly tenable. But there seems to
> be little to choose among the accounts. (Benacerraf, 1965, p. 284)

He thus concludes section II with the claim that numbers could not be sets
at all.

In his essay "What Mathematical Truth Could Not Be – I" (1996),
Benacerraf revisits his 1965 arguments (among other things). He notes:

> Most of the issues that are raised in the above argument [the argu-
> ment of sections I and II of Benacerraf (1965)] have received consid-
> erable discussion; very few, if any, have been satisfactorily resolved.
> (Benacerraf, 1996, p. 25)

He then considers the weaknesses of the argument. The first is that many
people (including Boolos, Dummett, and others) feel that the Frege-Russell
account or the Frege account of numbers as sets[10] did not receive due
consideration, and that one of these may indeed be the best candidate for
the natural numbers. The second weakness is that, in Benacerraf's words,
"no red-blooded realist ... should accept the bald statement that if there
isn't some *a priori* proof that some particular candidate reduction is the
correct one, there can't be a 'correct' one" (1996, p. 26).

The third weakness concerns what we ought to conclude from a successful reduction of entities of one type to entities of another. The argument of
sections I and II of "What Numbers Could Not Be" is directed primarily at
reductionists who are not inclined to deny the existence of entities that have
been successfully reduced to entities of another kind. Benacerraf likens this
type of reduction to packing for a trip to the tropics in which your taking of
only one sweater is not to deny the existence of the others you own; it's just
that you won't need them. That is, by reducing the natural numbers to

---

[10] On these accounts, the number three, for instance, is identified with the equivalence
class of all three-membered sets.

some set theoretic structure, all that is to be concluded is that we could do without the numbers since we have an isomorphic copy of them. The numbers are not ruled out of the catalogue of the "furniture of the universe" by such a reduction. Compare this with the thoroughgoing Ockhamist (such as Quine or Field), whose test for inclusion in the aforementioned catalogue is whether the entity in question is necessary for our best theories of the world (considered holistically). The argument of sections I and II of "What Numbers Could Not Be" does not have any impact on this latter position since "the holistic Ockhamite ... is not beholden to any notion of 'getting it right' that transcends the best theory" (Benacerraf, 1996, p. 27). These three weaknesses suggest three lines of attack on the argument, and of these Benacerraf has most sympathy with the first: defending the Frege-Russell analysis of natural number as the "right one."

There is, however, another possible reply to the argument of sections I and II of "What Numbers Could Not Be." Ironically, this reply is motivated by some of Benacerraf's remarks in the third section of this same essay. Benacerraf considers the question of what reductions of numbers to certain sequences of sets is supposed to show. He suggests that such reductions do not show that numbers are really sets after all, any more than the reduction of the natural numbers to certain sequences of oranges shows that natural numbers are really oranges. Benacerraf then combines this move with other (structuralist) assumptions to conclude that numbers cannot be objects at all. (I'll discuss this argument shortly.) I too have considerable sympathy with resisting the view that numbers are sets, but I wish to point out that this view can be used to motivate a quite different conclusion to that which Benacerraf draws. If one denies that the natural numbers are sets, then they may plausibly be sui generis objects. Thus one can admit that natural numbers can be modelled in set theory, but that this gives no reason to believe that numbers are sets. Benacerraf's indeterminacy argument has no force against such a position.

In the third section of "What Numbers Could Not Be" Benacerraf pushes the point a little further and argues for the conclusion that "not only could numbers not be sets, they couldn't even be numbers" (1965, p. 23). This he argues from two assumptions: (1) the structuralist premise that arithmetic is the science of progressions (not a particular progression, but progressions in general), and (2) the claim that no (particular) system of objects could exhibit only structural properties. The thought is that arithmetic is concerned only with the structural properties of the natural numbers.[11] Then Benacerraf considers what sorts of objects could have

[11] It should also be pointed out that this structuralist assumption provides a rather good reply to the arguments of the first two sections of Benacerraf (1965). According to

only structural properties and no intrinsic properties.[12] He (rather tentatively)[13] concludes that there can be no such objects because he believes
that all legitimate objects must have *some* non-structural properties.

In response to this argument I wish to make a couple of points. First,
it is clear that this argument has force only against structuralists. That is,
one could resist the argument by rejecting the structuralist premise that
there is nothing more to being the natural number n than being the nth
member of a sequence of objects. But even accepting structuralism, there
are at least two alternatives available. One is to deny (2), that is, to assert
the possibility of objects that have only structural properties. Such entities
would be rather strange and unlike any of the usual entities we come across
in our daily lives, but we already know that numbers are unlike the more
mundane entities we encounter, so such an appeal to weirdness has little
force. I don't wish to endorse such a view, nor do I wish to argue for it in
any detail. I'm merely flagging it as a possible structuralist response.

The other structuralist alternative to the argument of section III is
to take a more radical structuralist position. On this view, the objects of
mathematics are not the individual entities but, rather, the structures taken
as wholes. So, for example, the objects of arithmetic are not the individual
numbers, but the whole structure that is the natural-number ω-sequence—
the numbers themselves are merely *positions* in this structure. Again, I
don't wish to defend this view; I just offer it as a possible solution.[14]

There are, it seems, a variety of options available to the indispensabilist
for both the indeterminacy argument of sections I and II and for the more
sweeping claims of section III of Benacerraf (1965). Indeed, numbers could
be a variety of things (including sui generis entities) and the indispensability
argument doesn't legislate against many of these at all.

---

structuralism, questions that draw our attention to the differences between any two set-
theoretic reductions of the natural numbers are ruled out. For instance, the question "Is
$1 \in 3$?" (which is answered in the affirmative on Zermelo's account and in the negative
on von Neumann's) is ruled out as a non-structural question. (Note that this is different
from the solution I suggested on page 149.)

[12] There are many different accounts of intrinsic properties. My reference here is
simply to *non-relational properties*.

[13] Benacerraf (1996) points out that section III of "What Numbers Could Not Be"
has been much misunderstood. The conclusions of section III were being advanced with
much less confidence than those of the previous two sections, as they depend on the
rather controversial premises (1) and (2).

[14] See Michael Resnik's (1997) and Stewart Shapiro's (1997) for defences of views
along these lines.

7.2.2   Naturalising Mathematical Epistemology

In "Mathematical Truth" (1973) Benacerraf challenges philosophers of mathematics to: (1) naturalise mathematical epistemology, and (2) produce a semantics for mathematics that meshes with that of the rest of language. On a Platonist account of mathematics the second challenge is met easily since a proposition such as "there exists a prime number greater than 3" is made true by the existence of the number 5 (among others), just as "there exists a city larger than Melbourne" is made true by the existence of New York City (among others). The problem for Platonism, however, is to provide a naturalised account of mathematical epistemology. Benacerraf also shows how various anti-realist views of mathematical entities meet the first challenge but not the second. However, it is Benacerraf's challenge to Platonism that "Mathematical Truth" is best remembered for.

Benacerraf explicitly invokes the causal theory of knowledge as an ally in setting up the epistemological problem for Platonism (emphasis in original):

> I favor a causal account of knowledge on which for X to know that S is true requires some causal relation to obtain between X and the referents of the names, predicates, and quantifiers of S. I believe in addition in a causal theory of *reference*, thus making the link to my saying knowingly that S *doubly* causal. (Benacerraf, 1973, p. 412)

It is not surprising then that acausal mathematical entities have trouble on such an account. They can neither be referred to nor known about. Since 1973, when "Mathematical Truth" was first published,[15] causal theories of knowledge have fallen on hard times.[16] I won't rehearse the arguments against causal theories here (I discussed some of them in chapter 3).[17] It is sufficient to note that Benacerraf's challenge to Platonism explicitly depends on a now largely discredited epistemology.[18] That ought to be the end of the matter, but alas it's not. Despite the demise of the causal theory of knowledge, there remains considerable unease among many philosophers

---

[15] Although this essay was fairly widely known and circulated as early as 1968 (Benacerraf, 1996, p. 10).

[16] See Shope (1983) for a detailed account of their demise. Ironically one of the more important blows to causal theories came in 1973—the same year as "Mathematical Truth" was published—with Mark Steiner's "Platonism and the Causal Theory of Knowledge" (1973). See also Steiner's *Mathematical Knowledge* (1975), especially chapter 4.

[17] Perhaps their biggest failing is that they do not solve the Gettier problems that motivated them.

[18] Penelope Maddy (1996b, pp. 63–64) suggests that Benacerraf's challenge also depends on the correspondence theory of truth and that this too has been seriously challenged by disquotational accounts of truth.

over the prospects of a naturalised epistemology for mathematics. For instance, W. D. Hart writes:

> [I]t is a crime against the intellect to try to mask the problem of naturalizing the epistemology of mathematics with philosophical razzle-dazzle. Superficial worries about the intellectual hygiene of causal theories of knowledge are irrelevant to and misleading from this problem, for the problem is not so much about causality as about the very possibility of natural knowledge of abstract objects. (Hart, 1977, pp. 125–126)

What is it about Benacerraf's problem that allows it to outlive its major premise (and perhaps *both* its explicit premises[19])? As Maddy suggests, "there is a certain undeniable fascination to a problem so resilient!" (1996b, p. 64).

Hartry Field suggests that Benacerraf's problem for Platonism may be restated as a problem of explaining the *reliability* of our mathematical beliefs (emphasis in original):

> Benacerraf's challenge—or at least, the challenge which his paper suggests to me—is to provide an account of the mechanisms that explain how our beliefs about these remote entities can so well reflect the facts about them. The idea is that *if it appears in principle impossible to explain this*, then that tends to *undermine* the belief in mathematical entities, *despite* whatever reasons we might have for believing in them. Of course, the reasons for believing in mathematical entities (in particular, the indispensability arguments) still need to be addressed, but the role of the Benacerrafian challenge (as I see it) is to raise the cost of thinking that the postulation of mathematical entities is a proper solution, and thereby increase the motivation for showing that mathematics is not really indispensable after all. (Field, 1989, p. 26)

This formulation of Benacerraf's problem does not depend on the causal theory of knowledge. Indeed, as Field is quick to point out, it doesn't depend on *any* theory of knowledge (1988, pp. 232–233). I thus take Field's formulation to be a vast improvement on the original. In fact, I take Field's formulation (or something like it) to be the only formulation of Benacerraf's problem worthy of serious consideration today. How might an indispensabilist respond to this challenge?

The short answer is that the indispensability argument tells us that we come by mathematical knowledge in exactly the same way as other forms

---

[19] Cf. footnote 18.

of knowledge—by the hypothetico-deductive methods of science (Quine, 1969a). How is it that this method is a reliable process? That's a good question, but it's not one that the mathematical realist need be embarrassed by. This is a question that Platonists and nominalists alike must answer. The point of the original Benacerraf challenge and also Field's reformulation is to create a problem for Platonism. To ask after the reliability of the hypothetico-deductive method does not serve this purpose—it's either a problem for everyone or a problem for noone. Field concedes this possibility (emphasis in original):

> One could argue ... that if mathematics is indispensable to laws of empirical science, then *if the mathematical facts were different, different empirical consequences could be derived from the same laws of (mathematized) physics.* So, it could be said, mathematical facts make an empirical difference, and maybe this would enable the application-based platonist to argue that our observations of the empirical consequences of physical law are enough to explain the reliability of our mathematical beliefs. (Field, 1989, pp. 28–29)

Notice that this line of response depends on mathematics being contingent. But as I've already stated (in section 6.4), this is the most plausible position for an indispensabilist to take in any case.

Field, however, has some reservations about this line of response to Benacerraf's challenge. In particular, he is concerned that, given the relatively small amount of mathematics required for empirical science, this line of reasoning does not explain the reliability of very many of our mathematical beliefs.[20] We have seen this problem before in the guise of Maddy's claim that the Quinean indispensability argument leaves too much mathematics unaccounted for,[21] and the answer I will give here is essentially the same as I gave in response to Maddy: The reliability of our mathematical beliefs may be explained by their applicability to other areas of mathematics, so long as there is a chain of applications that leads eventually to empirical evidence. Such is the nature of applicability in the Quinean, holistic view of science. While I doubt that this response will *entirely* satisfy Field, it certainly weakens his point. At the very least, I believe that an appeal to applications in order to explain the reliability of our mathematical beliefs seems a promising avenue to investigate in reply to the Field formulation of the Benacerraf challenge.

---

[20] He also comments that the partial success of his nominalisation program exacerbates the situation by reducing the amount of mathematics required by empirical science (Field, 1989, p. 29).

[21] See section 5.1.3, for details.

Perhaps you are unsatisfied with the whole "short answer" approach to the Benacerraf challenge. Perhaps you'd like to hear more about the nature of the process that connects the *individual* abstract entities and our knowledge of them. Quine is unwilling to say any more than what I've said here. I too am inclined to think that questions about the process connecting the abstract objects and knowledge of them are misguided. Such questions yearn for causal answers and, as we have already seen, causal accounts of knowledge are generally considered untenable.

Gideon Rosen (1992, chapter 3) also subscribes to the view that such questions are misguided.[22] He points out that the Benacerraf challenge asks for justification of our mathematical beliefs one at a time. According to the indispensability argument, though, mathematical beliefs (indeed, *all* beliefs) are justified holistically. Someone who subscribes to this argument believes in mathematical entities because of the role they play in our total theory. Such a person should feel no compulsion to justify mathematical beliefs individually, and any demand that he or she do so is entirely unreasonable.[23]

The question of whether Quinean indispensabilists have a satisfactory answer to Benacerraf's challenge is a difficult and complicated matter. I hope, however, that I've shown that the Quinean has *an answer* to the challenge. (For what it's worth, I think that it's a *good* answer, but I don't expect that I've said enough here to convince the disbelievers.) Anyway, I won't pursue this issue further. Instead, I'd like to close with a few remarks about the use of indispensability arguments outside the philosophy of mathematics. In particular, I'd like to say a little about the use of indispensability arguments to motivate belief in concrete, non-actual possible worlds. Although such arguments have no *direct* bearing on the central topic of this book, they are worth a mention, since some philosophers feel

---

[22] It is difficult to track down *explicit* formulations of the following argument. I learnt it from Linsky and Zalta (1995, p. 528), who present the argument without endorsement and they (erroneously) attributed it to Burgess (1990). The argument may be found *implicitly* in Burgess and Rosen (1997, pp. 41–49) as well as in much of Quine's work. The only explicit formulations, with endorsement, I'm aware of are in Rosen's PhD thesis (1992) and in an unpublished manuscript by Smart.

[23] Some indispensabilists, however, may *choose* to say more about mathematical epistemology. What is said will obviously depend on the details of what he or she believes mathematical entities to be. For example, someone like the Maddy of *Realism in Mathematics* (1990a) can give a fully causal account of mathematical knowledge since, according to this view, we have causal contact with mathematical objects such as sets. John Bigelow (1988) also provides a causal story. Mark Balaguer (1995; 1998) suggests that if you are a "plentitudinous Platonist," that is, someone who believes in *all* the mathematical entities that could possibly exist, then the Benacerraf challenge is also met. Bernard Linsky and Ed Zalta (1995) make a similar proposal.

a slippery slope beckoning when they consider mathematical indispensability arguments.

7.3 A Slippery Slope?

David Lewis is clearly a believer in indispensability arguments, arguing, as he does, for concrete, causally isolated possible worlds on the basis of the usefulness of the possible worlds hypothesis:

> Why believe in a plurality of worlds?—Because the hypothesis is serviceable, and that is a reason to think that it is true. The familiar analysis of necessity as truth at all possible worlds was only the beginning. In the last two decades, philosophers have offered a great many more analyses that make reference to possible worlds, or to possible individuals that inhabit possible worlds. I find that record most impressive. I think it is clear that talk of *possibilia* has clarified questions in many parts of the philosophy of logic, of mind, of language, and of science—not to mention metaphysics itself. (Lewis, 1986b, p. 3)

Even disregarding Lewis's claims about the utility of possible-worlds talk for philosophical and logical purposes, it might be argued that the use of such talk in science alone is enough to justify the acceptance of possible worlds by a Quinean indispensabilist (who accepts the purposes of science as legitimate purposes for an indispensability argument).[24] Now if this is correct and if modal realism is considered unpalatable, it places the Quinean indispensabilist in an awkward situation. (Indeed, I've heard it said that this is a reductio ad absurdum of indispensability theory.)

I have two things to say in response to this concern. First, the indispensabilist's hands are not tied here. Ockhamist concerns might be invoked to put weight behind some of the alternative proposals for dealing with *possibilia* (such as modal fictionalism). Second, possible worlds do not find themselves in the same demand as mathematical entities. After all, most science gets by quite nicely without possible worlds, whereas the same is certainly not true of mathematical entities. From this it might be argued that possible worlds are not in fact indispensable. At the very least, the

---

[24] The scientific use of possible-worlds talk is many and varied. Phase planes are best described as spaces of possible initial conditions (and thus, arguably, implicitly invoke possible worlds). Possible worlds have been *explicitly* invoked to account for certain problems in quantum mechanics concerning the collapse of the wave function and also in cosmology to account for the so-called fine-tuning problem (Campbell, 1994, pp. 37–38).

prospect of denying the indispensability of possible worlds talk on such grounds seems to be an avenue worth exploring.

To be quite honest, I have no firm opinion on this matter. I grant that possible worlds talk is very useful and perhaps even indispensable. On the other hand, such talk is counterintuitive and leads to a very large ontology. One thing is clear: indispensability theory does not rule out modal realism a priori. Some see this itself as a problem, but I take it to be one of the most attractive features of indispensability theory. In fact, I'm highly suspicious of any methodological principle that rules against the existence of possible worlds (or whatever) on purely a priori grounds. There is nothing inconsistent about modal realism so, at the very least, we must be able to *entertain* this thesis. Indispensability theory allows this. Whether possible worlds make it into our ontology is another matter. But I hope it is clear by now that the Quine/Putnam indispensability argument does not purport to give easy answers to difficult questions; nor does it rule against interesting and fruitful theses without a fair trial. Surely this is as it should be.

Bibliography

Abell, G. O., Morrison, D., and Wolff, C. S. (1987). *Exploration of the Universe*, fifth edition. Philadelphia: Saunders College Publishing.

Ahlfors, L. V. (1966). *Complex Analysis*. New York: McGraw-Hill.

Armstrong, D. M. (1978). *Universals and Scientific Realism*. Cambridge: Cambridge University Press.

Armstrong, D. M. (1980). *The Nature of Mind*. Brighton, U.K.: Harvester Press.

Armstrong, D. M. (1980a). Naturalism materialism and first philosophy, in Armstrong (1980), pp. 149–165.

Armstrong, D. M. (1989). *A Combinatorial Theory of Possibility*. Cambridge: Cambridge University Press.

Azzouni, J. (1994). *Metaphysical Myths, Mathematical Practice: The Ontology and Epistemology of the Exact Sciences*. Cambridge: Cambridge University Press.

Azzouni, J. (1997a). Applied mathematics existential commitment and the Quine-Putnam indispensability thesis, *Philosophia Mathematica (3)*, 5(2), 193–227.

Azzouni, J. (1997b). Thick epistemic access: distinguishing the mathematical from the empirical, *Journal of Philosophy*, 94(9), 472–484.

Azzouni, J. (1998). On "on what there is," *Pacific Philosophical Quarterly*, 79(1), 1–18.

Azzouni, J. (2000). Stipulation logic and ontological independence, *Philosophia Mathematica (3)*, forthcoming.

Baker, A. R. (forthcoming). Mathematics indispensability and scientific progress, *Erkenntnis*.

Balaguer, M. (1995). A Platonist epistemology, *Synthese*, 103(3), 303–325.

Balaguer, M. (1996a). Towards a nominalization of quantum mechanics, *Mind*, 105(418), 209–226.

Balaguer, M. (1996b). A fictionalist account of the indispensable applications of mathematics, *Philosophical Studies*, 83, 291–314.

Balaguer, M. (1998). *Platonism and Anti-Platonism in Mathematics*, New York: Oxford University Press.

Barrow, J. D., and Tipler, F. J. (1996). *The Anthropic Cosmological Principle*. Oxford: Oxford University Press.

Beall, J. C. (2001). Existential claims and Platonism, *Philosophia Mathematica (3)*, 9, forthcoming.

Benacerraf, P. (1965). What numbers could not be, reprinted in Benacerraf and Putnam (1983), pp. 272–294 (first published in 1965).

Benacerraf, P. (1973). Mathematical truth, reprinted in Benacerraf and Putnam (1983), pp. 403–420 (first published in 1973).

Benacerraf, P., and Putnam, H. (eds.) (1983). *Philosophy of Mathematics Selected Readings*, second edition. Cambridge: Cambridge University Press.

Benacerraf, P. (1996). What mathematical truth could not be — I, in Morton and Stich (1996), pp. 9–59.

Bernstein, J. (1973). *Einstein*. Glasgow: Fontana/Collins.

Bigelow, J. (1988). *The Reality of Numbers: A Physicalist's Philosophy of Mathematics*. Oxford: Clarendon.

Bigelow, J., and Pargetter, R. (1990). *Science and Necessity*. Cambridge: Cambridge University Press.

Boyce, W. E., and DiPrima, R. C. (1986). *Elementary Differential Equations and Boundary Value Problems*, fourth edition. New York: John Wiley.

Burgess, J. (1983). Why I am not a nominalist, *Notre Dame Journal of Formal Logic*, 24(1), 93–105.

Burgess, J. (1990). Epistemology and nominalism, in Irvine (1990), pp. 1–15.

Burgess, J., and Rosen, G. (1997). *A Subject with No Object: Strategies for Nominalistic Interpretation of Mathematics*. Oxford: Clarendon, Oxford, 1997.

Campbell, K. (1994). Selective realism in the philosophy of physics, *The Monist*, 77, 27–46.

Carnap, R. (1937). *The Logical Syntax of Language*. London: Routledge and Kegan Paul.

Cartwright, N. (1983). *How the Laws of Physics Lie*. New York: Oxford University Press.

Cheyne, C. (1998). Existence claims and causality, *Australasian Journal of Philosophy*, 76(1), 34–47.

Cheyne, C., and Pigden, C. (1996). Pythagorean powers or a challenge to Platonism, *Australasian Journal of Philosophy*, 74(4), 639–645.

Chihara, C. S. (1973). *Ontology and the Vicious-Circle Principle*. Ithaca, NY: Cornell University Press.

Chihara, C. S. (1990). *Constructibility and Mathematical Existence*. Oxford: Clarendon.

Colyvan, M. (1998a). In defence of indispensability, *Philosophia Mathematica (3)*, 6(1), 39–62.

Colyvan, M. (1998b). Is Platonism a bad bet? *Australasian Journal of Philosophy*, 76(1), 115–119.

Colyvan, M. (1998c). Can the Eleatic principle be justified? *Canadian Journal of Philosophy*, 28(3), 313–336.

Colyvan, M. (1999a). Review of Maddy, P. *Naturalism in Mathematics*, *Mind*, 108(431), 586–590.

Colyvan, M. (1999b). Contrastive empiricism and indispensability, *Erkenntnis*, 51(2–3), 323–332.

Colyvan, M. (1999c). Confirmation theory and indispensability, *Philosophical Studies*, 96(1), 1–19.

Colyvan, M. (2000). Conceptual contingency and abstract existence, *Philosophical Quarterly*, 50(198), 87–91.

Colyvan, M., and Zalta, E. N. (1999). Mathematics: truth and fiction? *Philosophia Mathematica (3)*, 7(3), 336–349.

Dales, H. G., and Oliveri, G. (eds.) (1998). *Truth in Mathematics*. Oxford: Clarendon.

Dancy, J., and Sosa, E. (eds.) (1992). *A Companion to Epistemology*. Oxford: Blackwell.

Devlin, K. (1977). *The Axiom of Constructibility*, Lecture Notes in Mathematics, Vol. 617. Berlin: Springer-Verlag.

d'Inverno, R. (1992). *Introducing Einstein's Relativity*. Oxford: Clarendon.

Dirac, P. A. M. (1958). *The Principles of Quantum Mechanics*, fourth edition (revised). Oxford: Clarendon.

Dowe, P. (1997). A defence of backwards-in-time causation models in quantum mechanics, *Synthese*, 112, 233–246.

Duhem, P. (1906). *The Aim and Structure of Physical Theory*. Princeton: Princeton University Press, 1954 (first published in 1906).

Dummett, M. (1975). The philosophical basis of intuitionistic logic, reprinted in Benacerraf and Putnam (1983), pp. 97–129 (first published in 1975).

Dummett, M. (1978). *Truth and Other Enigmas*. London: Duckworth.

Dummett, M. (1978a). Realism, in Dummett (1978), pp. 145–165.

Dummett, M. (1991). *Frege: Philosophy of Mathematics*. London: Duckworth.

Dyson, F. J. (1964). Mathematics in the physical sciences, *Scientific American*, 211(3), 128–146.

Einstein, A. (1905). On the electrodynamics of moving bodies, reprinted in Einstein et al. (1923), pp. 35–65 (first published in 1905).

Einstein, A. (1967). *The Meaning of Relativity*, sixth edition. London: Chapman and Hall.

Einstein, A., Lorentz, H. A., Weyl, H., and Minkowski, H. (1923). *The Principle of Relativity*. New York: Dover.

Ellis, B. (1990). *Truth and Objectivity*. Oxford: Blackwell.

Enderton, H. B. (1977). *Elements of Set Theory*. New York: Academic Press.

Feynman, R. (1965). *The Character of Physical Law*. London: BBC.

Feynman, R., Leighton, R., and Sands, M. (1963). *The Feynman Lectures on Physics*. Reading, Mass.: Addison-Wesley.

Field, H. (1980). *Science Without Numbers: A Defence of Nominalism*. Oxford: Blackwell.

Field, H. (1984). Can we dispense with space-time? reprinted in Field (1989), pp. 171–226 (first published in 1984).

Field, H. (1985). On conservativeness and incompleteness, reprinted in Field (1989), pp. 125–146 (first published in 1985).

Field, H. (1988). Realism mathematics and modality, reprinted in Field (1989), pp. 227–281 (first published in 1988).

Field, H. (1989). *Realism, Mathematics and Modality*. Oxford: Blackwell.

Field, H. (1990). Mathematics without truth (a reply to Maddy), *Pacific Philosophical Quarterly*, 71(3), 206–222.

Field, H. (1992). A nominalistic proof of the conservativeness of set theory, *Journal of Philosophical Logic*, 21(2), 111–123.

Field, H. (1993). The conceptual contingency of mathematical objects, *Mind*, 102(406), 285–299.

Fodor, J., and Lepore, E. (1992). *Holism: A Shopper's Guide*. Cambridge: Blackwell.

Forrest, P., and Armstrong, D. M. (1987). The nature of number, *Philosophical Papers*, 16, 165–186.

Frege, G. (translated by Austin, J. L.) (1884). *The Foundations of Arithmetic: A Logico-mathematical enquiry into the concept of number*, Oxford: Blackwell, 1950 (first published in 1884).

Frege, G. (edited by Geach, P., and Black, M.) (1970). *Translations from the Philosophical Writings of Gottlob Frege*. Cambridge: Blackwell.

Glymour, C. (1980). *Theory and Evidence*. Princeton: Princeton University Press.

Gödel, K. (1947). What is Cantor's continuum problem? reprinted (revised and expanded) in Benacerraf and Putnam (1983), pp. 470–485 (first published in 1947).

Grice, H. P., and Strawson, P. F. (1956). In defence of a dogma, *Philosophical Review*, LXV, 141–158.

Hacking, I. (1983). *Representing and Intervening*. Cambridge: Cambridge University Press.

Hahn, L., and Schilpp, P. (eds.) (1986). *The Philosophy of W.V. Quine*. La Salle, Ill.: Open Court.

Hale, R. (1987). *Abstract Objects*. Oxford: Blackwell.

Hale, R., and Wright, C. (1992). Nominalism and the contingency of abstract objects, *Journal of Philosophy*, 89(3), 111–135.

Hale, R., and Wright, C. (1994). A reductio ad surdum?: Field on the contingency of mathematical objects, *Mind*, 103(410), 169–184.

Hardy, G .H. (1940). *A Mathematician's Apology*. Cambridge: Cambridge University Press, 1967 (first published in 1940).

Hart, W. D. (1977). Review of Steiner's *Mathematical Knowledge*, *Journal of Philosophy*, 74, 118–129.

Hart, W. D. (ed.) (1996). *The Philosophy of Mathematics*. Oxford: Oxford University Press.

Hellman, G. (1989). *Mathematics Without Numbers: Towards a Modal-Structural Interpretation*. Oxford: Clarendon.

Hellman, G. (1992). The boxer and his fists: the constructivist in the arena of quantum physics, *Proceedings of the Aristotelian Society, Supplement, LXVI*, 61–77.

Hellman, G. (1999). Some ins and outs of indispensability: a modal-structural perspective, in Cantini, A., Casari, E., and Minari, P. (eds.) *Logic and Foundations of Mathematics*. Dordrecht: Kluwer, pp. 25–39.

Hempel, C. G. (1965). *Aspects of Scientific Explanation and Other Essays in the Philosophy of Science*. London: Macmillan.

Heyting, A. (1931). The intuitionistic foundations of mathematics, reprinted in Benacerraf and Putnam (1983), pp. 52–61 (first published in 1931).

Hilbert, D. (1899). *Foundations of Geometry*. La Salle, Ill.: Open Court, 1971 (first published in 1899).

Horwich, P. (1982). *Probability and Evidence*. Cambridge: Cambridge University Press.

Irvine, A. D. (ed.) (1990). *Physicalism in Mathematics*. Dordrecht: Kluwer.

Jackson, F. (1998). *From Metaphysics to Ethics: A Defence of Conceptual Analysis*. Oxford: Clarendon.

Jackson, F., and Pettit, P. (1990). Program explanation: a general perspective, *Analysis*, 50, 107–117.

Kitcher, P. (1981). Explanatory unification, *Philosophy of Science*, 48, 507–531.

Kitcher, P. (1984). *The Nature of Mathematical Knowledge*. New York: Oxford University Press.

Kline, M. (1972). *Mathematical Thought from Ancient to Modern Times*. New York: Oxford University Press.

Kosniowski, C. (1980). *A First Course in Algebraic Topology*. Cambridge: Cambridge University Press.

Kripke, S. (1980). *Naming and Necessity*. Oxford: Blackwell.

Lakatos, I. (1970). Falsification and the methodology of scientific research programmes, in Lakatos, I., and Musgrave, A. (eds.) *Criticism and the Growth of Knowledge*, Cambridge: Cambridge University Press, pp. 91–195.

Lakatos, I. (1976). *Proofs and Refutations: The Logic of Mathematical Discovery*. Cambridge: Cambridge University Press.

Lewis, D. (1986). *Philosophical Papers Vol. II*. New York: Oxford University Press.

Lewis, D. (1986a). Causal explanation, in Lewis (1986), pp. 214–240.

Lewis, D. (1986b). *On the Plurality of Worlds*. Oxford: Blackwell.

Lewis, D. (1991). *Parts of Classes*. Oxford: Blackwell.

Linsky, B. (unpublished). Placing abstract objects in naturalism.

Linsky, B., and Zalta, E. N. (1995). Naturalized Platonism versus Platonized naturalism, *Journal of Philosophy*, 92(10), 525–555.

Lorentz, H. A. (1885). Michelson's interference experiment, reprinted in Einstein et al. (1923), pp. 1–7 (first published in 1885).

Lorentz, H. A. (1904). Electromagnetic phenomena in a system moving with any velocity less than that of light, reprinted in Einstein et al. (1923), pp. 9–34 (first published in 1904).

Maddy, P. (1990a). *Realism in Mathematics*. Oxford: Clarendon.

Maddy, P. (1990b). Physicalistic Platonism, in Irvine (1990), pp. 259–289.

Maddy. P. (1990c). Mathematics and Oliver Twist, *Pacific Philosophical Quarterly*, 71(3), 189–205.

Maddy, P. (1992). Indispensability and practice, *Journal of Philosophy*, 89(6), 275–289.

Maddy, P. (1994). Taking naturalism seriously, in Prawitz, D., Skyrms, B., and Westerståhl, D. (eds.) *Logic, Methodology and Philosophy of Science IX*. Amsterdam: Elsevier, pp. 383–407.

Maddy, P. (1995). Naturalism and ontology, *Philosophia Mathematica (3)*, 3(3), 248–270.

Maddy, P. (1996a). Set theoretic naturalism, *The Journal of Symbolic Logic*, 61(2), 490–514.

Maddy, P. (1996b). The legacy of "Mathematical Truth," in Morton and Stich (1996), pp. 60–72.

Maddy, P. (1996c). Ontological commitment: between Quine and Duhem, in Tomberlin, J. E. (ed.) *Philosophical Perspectives 10: Metaphysics 1996*. Oxford: Blackwell, pp. 317–341.

Maddy, P. (1997). *Naturalism in Mathematics*. Oxford: Clarendon.

Maddy, P. (1998a). Naturalizing mathematical methodology, in Schirn (1998), pp. 175–193.

Maddy, P. (1998b). How to be a naturalist about mathematics, in Dales and Oliveri (1998), pp. 161–180.

Malament, D. (1982). Review of Field's *Science Without Numbers*, *Journal of Philosophy*, 79, 523–534.

Martin, D. A. (1998). Mathematical evidence, in Dales and Oliveri (1998), pp. 215–231.

McCleary, J. (1994). *Geometry from a Differentiable Viewpoint*. Cambridge: Cambridge University Press.

Mill, J. S. (1843). *A System of Logic*, New impression. London: Longmans, Green and Co., 1947 (first published in 1843).

Morton, A., and Stich, S. P. (eds.) (1996). *Benacerraf and his Critics*. Oxford: Blackwell.

Musgrave, A. (1986). Arithmetical Platonism: Is Wright wrong or must Field yield? in Fricke, M. (ed.) *Essays in Honour of Bob Durrant*. Dunedin: Otago University Philosophy Department, 1986, pp. 90–110.

Oddie, G. (1982). Armstrong on the Eleatic principle and abstract entities, *Philosophical Studies* 41, 285–295.

Papineau, D. (1993). *Philosophical Naturalism*. Oxford: Blackwell.

Parsons, C. (1980). Mathematical intuition, reprinted in Hart (1996), pp. 95–113 (first published in 1980).

Parsons, C. (1983). *Mathematics in Philosophy*, Ithaca, NY: Cornell University Press.

Parsons, C. (1983a). Quine on the philosophy of mathematics, in Parsons (1983), pp. 176–205.

Peat, F. D. (1992). *Superstrings and the Search for the Theory of Everything*. London: Abacus.

Plato, (1935). Sophist, trans. Cornford, F. M. in *Plato's Theory of Knowledge*. London: Kegan Paul.

Price, H. (1996). *Time's Arrow and Archimedes' Point: New Directions for the Physics of Time*. Oxford: Oxford University Press.

Price, H. (1999). The role of history in microphysics, in Sankey, H. (ed.) *Causation and Laws of Nature*. Dordrecht: Kluwer, pp. 331-345.

Priest, G. (1979). Two dogmas of Quineanism, *Philosophical Quarterly*, 29(117), 289–301.

Priest, G. (1997). Inconsistent models of arithmetic part I: finite models, *Journal of Philosophical Logic*, 26(2), 223–235.

Putnam, H. (1967). Mathematics without foundations, reprinted in Putnam (1979), pp. 43–59 (first published in 1967).

Putnam, H. (1971). Philosophy of logic, reprinted in Putnam (1979), pp. 323–357 (first published in 1971).

Putnam, H. (1973). Reference and meaning, *Journal of Philosophy* 70, 699–711.

Putnam, H. (1976). Two dogmas revisited, reprinted in Putnam (1983), pp. 87–97 (first published in 1976).

Putnam, H. (1979). *Mathematics Matter and Method: Philosophical Papers Vol. I*, second edition. Cambridge: Cambridge University Press.

Putnam, H. (1979a). What is mathematical truth?, in Putnam (1979), pp. 60–78.

Putnam, H. (1979b). Analyticity and apriority: beyond Wittgenstein and Quine, reprinted in Putnam (1983), pp. 115–138 (first published in 1979).

Putnam, H. (1983). *Realism and Reason: Philosophical Papers Vol. 3*. Cambridge: Cambridge University Press.

Quine, W. V. (1936). Truth by convention, reprinted in Benacerraf and Putnam (1983), pp. 329–354 (first published in 1936).

Quine, W. V. (1948). On what there is, reprinted in Quine (1980), pp. 1–19 (first published 1948).

Quine, W. V. (1951). Two dogmas of empiricism, reprinted in Quine (1980), pp. 20–46 (first published in 1951).

Quine, W. V. (1953). On mental entities, reprinted in Quine (1976), pp. 221–227 (first published in 1953).

Quine, W. V. (1960). *Word and Object*. New York: Massachusetts Institute of Technology Press and John Wiley and Sons.

Quine, W. V. (1960a). Posits and reality, reprinted in Quine (1976), pp. 246–254 (first published in 1960).

Quine, W. V. (1963). Carnap and logical truth, reprinted in Benacerraf and Putnam (1983), pp. 355–376 (first published in 1963).

Quine, W. V. (1969). *Ontological Relativity and Other Essays*. New York: Columbia University Press.

Quine, W. V. (1969a). Epistemology naturalised, in Quine (1969), pp. 69–90.

Quine, W. V. (1969b). Existence and quantification, in Quine (1969), pp. 91–113.

Quine, W. V. (1974). *The Roots of Reference*. La Salle. Ill.: Open Court.

Quine, W. V. (1976). *The Ways of Paradox and Other Essays*, revised edition. Cambridge, Mass.: Harvard University Press.

Quine, W. V. (1980). *From a Logical Point of View*, second edition. Cambridge, Mass.: Harvard University Press, (first edition 1953).

Quine, W. V. (1981). *Theories and Things*. Cambridge, Mass.: Harvard University Press.

Quine, W. V. (1981a). Five milestones of empiricism, in Quine (1981), pp. 67–72.

Quine, W. V. (1981b). Success and limits of mathematization, in Quine (1981), pp. 148–155.

Quine, W. V. (1986). Reply to Charles Parsons, in Hahn and Schilpp (1986), pp. 396–403.

Quine, W. V. (1992). *Pursuit of Truth*, revised edition. Cambridge, Mass.: Harvard University Press (first edition 1990).

Quine, W. V. (1995). *From Stimulus to Science*. Cambridge, Mass.: Harvard University Press.

Resnik, M. D. (1981). Mathematics as a science of patterns: ontology and reference, *Noûs*, 15(4), 529–550.

Resnik, M. D. (1982). Mathematics as a science of patterns: epistemology, *Noûs*, 16(1), 95–105.

Resnik, M. D. (1983). Review of Hartry Field's *Science Without Numbers*, *Noûs*, 17, 514–519.

Resnik, M. D. (1985a). How nominalist is Hartry Field's nominalism? *Philosophical Studies*, 47, 163–181.

Resnik, M. D. (1985b). Ontology and logic: remarks on Hartry Field's anti-platonist philosophy of mathematics, *History and Philosophy of Logic*, 6, 191–209.

Resnik, M. D. (1995). Scientific vs. mathematical realism: the indispensability argument, *Philosophia Mathematica (3)*, 3(2), 166–174.

Resnik, M. D. (1997). *Mathematics as a Science of Patterns*. Oxford: Clarendon.

Resnik, M. D. (1998). Holistic mathematics, in Schirn (1998), chapter 9.

Riskin, A. (1994). On the most open question in the history of mathematics: a discussion of Maddy, *Philosophia Mathematica (3)*, 2(2), 109–121.

Rosen, G. (1992). Remarks on modern nominalism, PhD dissertation, Princeton University.

Roseveare, N. T. (1983). *Mercury's Perihelion from Le Verrier to Einstein*, Oxford: Clarendon.

Russell, B. (1920). *Introduction to Mathematical Philosophy*. New York: Dover, 1993 (first published in 1920).

Russell, B. (1924). Philosophy in the twentieth century, reprinted in *Sceptical Essays*, Sixth impression. London: George Allen and Unwin, 1956, pp. 54–79 (first published in 1924).

Sayre-McCord, G. (1988). Introduction: the many moral realisms, in Sayre-McCord, G. (ed.) *Moral Realism*. Ithaca, NY: Cornell University Press, pp. 1–26.

Schirn, M. (ed.) (1998). *Philosophy of Mathematics Today*. Oxford: Clarendon.

Shapiro, S. (1983). Conservativeness and incompleteness, *Journal of Philosophy*, 80(9), 521–531.

Shapiro, S. (1997). *Philosophy of Mathematics: Structure and Ontology*. Oxford: Oxford University Press.

Shope, R. (1983). *The Analysis of Knowing: A Decade of Research*. Princeton: Princeton University Press.

Singh, S. (1997). *Fermat's Last Theorem: The Story of a Riddle that Confounded the World's Greatest Minds for 358 Years*. London: Fourth Estate.

Smart, J. J. C. (1963). *Philosophy and Scientific Realism*. London: Routledge and Kegan Paul.

Smart, J. J. C. (1990). Explanation—opening address, Knowles, D. (ed.) *Explanation and its Limits*. Cambridge: Cambridge University Press, pp. 1–19.

Smart, J. J. C. (unpublished). Prospects for the philosophy of mathematics.

Sober, E. (1993). Mathematics and indispensability, *Philosophical Review*, 102(1), 35–57.

Steiner, M. (1973). Platonism and the causal theory of knowledge, *Journal of Philosophy* 70, 57–66.

Steiner, M. (1975). *Mathematical Knowledge*. Ithaca, NY: Cornell University Press.

Steiner, M. (1989). The application of mathematics to natural science, *Journal of Philosophy*, 86(9), 449–480.

Steiner, M. (1995). The applicabilities of mathematics, *Philosophia Mathematica (3)*, 3(2), 129–156.

Steiner, M. (1998). *The Applicability of Mathematics as a Philosophical Problem*, Cambridge, Mass.: Harvard University Press.

Urquhart, A. (1990). The logic of physical theory, in Irvine (1990), pp. 145–154.

van Fraassen, B. (1980). *The Scientific Image*. Oxford: Clarendon.

Wagner, S. J. (1996). Prospects for Platonism, in Morton and Stich (1996), pp. 73–99.

Weinberg, S. (1993). *Dreams of a Final Theory*. London: Vintage.

Wigner, E. P. (1960). The unreasonable effectiveness of mathematics in the natural sciences, *Communications on Pure and Applied Mathematics*, 13, 1–14.

Williams, D. C. (1944). Naturalism and the nature of things, reprinted in Williams, D. C. *Principles of Empirical Realism*. Springfield, Ill.: Charles Thomas, 1966, pp. 212–238 (first published 1944).

Wolszczan, A., and Frail, D. A. (1992). A planetary system around the millisecond pulsar PSR1257+12, *Nature*, 355 (9 January 1992), 145–147.

Wright, C. (1983). *Frege's Conception of Numbers as Objects*. Aberdeen: Aberdeen University Press.

Wright, C. (1988). Why numbers can believably be, *Revue Internationale de Philosophie*, 42, 425–473.

Wright, C. (1992). *Truth and Objectivity*. Cambridge, Mass.: Harvard University Press.

Index